1000 Lean and Green Ultimate Cookbook

1000-Day Fueling Hacks & Lean and Green Recipes to Help You Keep Healthy and Lose Weight. With 5 & 1 and 4 & 2 & 1 Meal Plan

Natalie Fremont

Table of Contents

Introduction

Do you want to try something new, different and effective to achieve good health and active metabolism? Then here comes a fairly new concept known as the Lean and green diet. This dietary regime takes a whole new approach and suggests weight loss through multiple measures taken at a time. The diet is essentially restrictive, and it also promotes the use of food fueling to compensate for the reduced caloric intake and to meet all the nutritional needs. Well, in this cookbook, you will learn all about the basic concept of the fueling based diet, the lean and green diet approach, and its different weight loss programs. There are various factors that work together to make the lean and green diet plan effective for weight loss; all such factors are thoroughly discussed in the first part of the book.

The content of this cookbook comes from my own experience of trying the lean and green diet and finding it quite effective for weight loss. I had never tried a meal replacement diet before, so for me, it was a first-hand experience of trying this weight loss program. Initially, I tried the 3x3 lean and green diet plan, and the results came out to be pretty satisfying. From that point, I tried its other plans as well. With Lean and green diet, I not only managed to lose some weight, but it brought me good health as well. Let's see how you can put this dietary approach up to its best use. The part of this book is designed you introduce the basics of the lean and green diet, where you will get to know about the lean and green meals and food that are suitable to prepare its weight loss meal plan. The second part of this book will provide you with several recipes to introduce and incorporate all the lean and green ingredients into your diet while adding a variety of flavours and aromas.

Lean and Green diet

Lean and green diet is basically a weight loss or weight maintenance program that suggests the use of a lean and green meal along with processed food called "fueling." The diet says to add these nutritional Fuelings to the diet while controlling the overall caloric intake. The fueling is actually powdered food, which is mixed with liquid like water and then added to the diet as a part of routine meals. Besides consuming these fueling, the dieters are also suggested to exercise 30 minutes daily to lose weight. By trying fueling as a substitute for real food, you can curb the carb and sugar intake and can manage your caloric intake as well. How much Fuelings to consume, how much food to eat, and what to eat on this dietary regime depends on the type of weight loss plan you are going for. However, on this diet, the overall calorie intake for adults is reduced to 800 to 1000 per day, which lets you lose about 12 lbs of weight per 12 weeks on average.

What do you eat on the lean and green diet?

The following are the food items that you can opt for on this diet plan:

1. Meat:

The lean and green diet only allows 85 per cent of lean meat on a diet; whether it is chicken, beef, turkey, lamb, pork, and ground meat, it all has to be lean. Lean meat has lower fat content, which makes it great to keep the caloric intake in control.

2. Seafood:

Seafood is best to have on any weight loss regime because it is free from saturated fats and brings a lot of nutritional value to the table. You can have all types of fishes and seafood on this diet, including halibut, salmon, trout, lobster, tuna, shrimp, crab, and scallops, etc.

3. Eggs:

Eggs are rich in protein, and they are low in carbs; that's what makes eggs the right for this diet.

4. Soy products:

In soy products, tofu is the only product that is allowed on the lean and green diet because it is processed, and the caloric content is suitable for the lean diet.

5. Fats:

Not all fats are healthy, and there are a handful of options that you must try on this diet that includes most of the vegetable olive oil, walnut oil, canola oil, flaxseed oil. Other fats sources that can be incorporated into this diet include nuts and seeds, reduced-fat margarine, and olives.

6. Low carb vegetables:

All low-carb vegetables are a suitable fit for the Lean and green diet. So, except potatoes, yams, sweet potatoes, yellow squash, and beetroots, you can try every other vegetable on this diet, including spinach, cabbage, collard greens, cucumbers, mushrooms, celery, onion, tomatoes, garlic, ginger, eggplant, cauliflower, broccoli, bell peppers, zucchini, and spaghetti squash, etc.

7. Sugar-free snacks:

Snacks are usually loaded with carbs and sugar, so they must be avoided most of the time. But you have snacks in some amounts, then only try the sugar-free and low-carb snacks.

8. Sugar-free beverages:

In beverages, there are limited options as well. For the most part of this diet, water is the most recommended drink since it is zero caloric and comes with several health advantages. Besides that, you can have unsweetened almond milk, coconut milk, sugar-free tea, coffee

9. Condiments and seasonings:

In condiments and seasonings, there are no such restrictions; from dried herbs to salt, lemon juice, ground and whole spices, lime juice, yellow mustard, soy sauce, and salsa, you can use any. Whereas in syrups and sauces, stay from the sugar-rich varieties and try the sugar-free syrups, low-carb sweeteners, sugar-free ketchup and barbecue sauce, etc.

Foods to avoid

• All fried foods are off the list for the lean and green diet, whether it is the fried fish, meat, poultry, fruits, vegetables, or fried desserts.

• The high carb refined grain items are also not a suitable option for this diet; such products include pasta, white bread, flour tortillas, biscuits, pancakes crackers, white rice, cakes, cookies, pastries, and other similar baked goods.

• Saturated fats from butter or solid shortening are also not the right fit for this diet.

• Milk, yogurt, and cheese are termed whole-fat dairy items, and they must also be avoided.

• All varieties of alcohol are strictly forbidden on this diet.

• All sweetened beverages like soda drinks, sports drinks, fruit juices, energy drinks, flavored milk, and sweetened tea, etc., are also not allowed for this diet.

Fueling Hacks Recipes

Lean and Green Smoothie

Prep Time: 5 minutes.
Cook Time: 0 minutes.
Serves: 2

Ingredients:

- 2 ½ cups kale leaves, stemmed
- 1 cup pineapple, cubed
- ¾ cup apple juice, chilled
- ½ cup seedless green grapes, frozen
- ½ cup Granny Smith apple, chopped
- 1 cup green grapes, halved

Preparation:

1. Blend kale with grapes with apple and pineapple in a blender.
2. Serve with halved grapes.
3. Enjoy.

Serving Suggestion: Enjoy this smoothie with breakfast muffins.

Variation Tip: Add some strawberries to the smoothie.

Nutritional Information Per Serving:

Calories 84 | Fat 7.9g |Sodium 704mg | Carbs 19g | Fiber 2g | Sugar 14g | Protein 1g

Medifast Patties

Prep Time: 10 minutes.
Cook Time: 20 minutes.
Serves: 4

Ingredients:

- 1 3/4 lbs. Dungeness crab meat
- 1 tablespoon red bell pepper, diced
- 1 tablespoon green bell pepper, diced
- 1 tablespoon parsley leaves, chopped
- 1 ½ tablespoon heavy mayonnaise
- 2 eggs 3 teaspoons baking powder
- 1 teaspoon Worcestershire sauce
- 1 teaspoon Old Bay seasoning
- 10 cooking spray

Preparation:

1. Mix crab meat with bell peppers, parsley, mayonnaise, baking powder, Worcestershire sauce and old bay seasoning in a bowl.
2. Make small patties out of this mixture.
3. Set a skillet, greased with cooking spray, over medium heat.
4. Sear the patties for 5 minutes per side.
5. Enjoy.

Serving Suggestion: Serve these patties with toasted bread slices.

Variation Tip: Add chopped carrots and broccoli to the cakes.

Nutritional Information Per Serving:
Calories 214 | Fat 5.1g |Sodium 231mg | Carbs 31g | Fiber 5g | Sugar 2.1g | Protein 17g

Green Colada Smoothie

Prep Time: 5 minutes.
Cook Time: 0 minutes.
Serves: 2

Ingredients:

- 1 cup Greek yogurt
- 1 cup frozen pineapple
- 1 cup baby spinach
- ½ cup lite coconut milk
- ½ teaspoon vanilla extract
- Coconut flakes for garnish

Preparation:

1. Blend yogurt with pineapple, spinach, coconut milk, and vanilla in a blender until smooth.
2. Garnish with coconut flakes and serve.

Serving Suggestion: Enjoy this smoothie with breakfast muffins.

Variation Tip: Add some strawberries to the smoothie.

Nutritional Information Per Serving:
Calories 325 | Fat 9g |Sodium 118mg | Carbs 35.4g | Fiber 2.9g | Sugar 15g | Protein 26.5g

Green Apple Smoothie

Prep Time: 5 minutes.
Cook Time: 0 minutes.
Serves: 2

Ingredients:

- 2 ripe bananas
- 1 ripe pear, peeled, chopped
- 2 cups kale leaves, chopped
- ½ cup of orange juice
- ½ cup of cold water
- 12 ice cubes
- 1 tablespoon ground flaxseed

Preparation:

1. Blend bananas with pear, kale leaves, orange juice, cold water, ice cubes and flaxseed in a blender.
2. Serve.

Serving Suggestion: Serve this smoothie with morning muffins.

Variation Tip: Add some strawberries to the smoothie.

Nutritional Information Per Serving:
Calories 213 | Fat 2.5g |Sodium 15.6mg | Carbs 49.5g | Fiber 7.6g | Sugar 28g | Protein 3.5g

Spinach Smoothie

Prep Time: 5 minutes.
Cook Time: 0 minutes.
Serves: 2

Ingredients:

- 1 cup fresh spinach
- 1 banana
- ½ green apple
- 4 hulled strawberries
- 4 (1 inch) pieces frozen mango
- ⅓ cup whole milk
- 1 scoop vanilla protein powder
- 1 teaspoon honey

Preparation:

1. Blend spinach with banana with the green apple with strawberries, mango, milk, protein powder and honey in a blender.
2. Serve.

Serving Suggestion: Enjoy this smoothie with breakfast muffins.

Variation Tip: Add some blueberries to the smoothie.

Nutritional Information Per Serving:
Calories 312 | Fat 25g |Sodium 132mg | Carbs 44g | Fiber 3.9g | Sugar 3g | Protein 18.9g

Kale and Cheese Muffins

Prep Time: 10 minutes.
Cook Time: 25 minutes.
Serves: 9

Ingredients:

- 9 large eggs
- 1 cup liquid egg whites
- 3/4 cup plain Greek yogurt
- 2 ounces goat cheese crumbled
- 1/2 teaspoon salt
- 10 ounces kale
- 2 cups cherry tomatoes
- cooking spray

Preparation:

1. At 375 degrees F, preheat your oven.
2. Beat eggs with goat cheese, yogurt, and egg whites in a bowl.
3. Stir in cherry tomatoes and kale, then divide this mixture into a muffin tray.
4. Bake the muffin cups for 25 minutes in the preheated oven.
5. Enjoy.

Serving Suggestion: Serve these muffins with a green smoothie.

Variation Tip: Add chopped nuts to the batter.

Nutritional Information Per Serving:
Calories 290 | Fat 15g |Sodium 595mg | Carbs 11g | Fiber 3g | Sugar 12g | Protein 29g

Matcha Avocado Smoothie

Prep Time: 5 minutes.
Cook Time: 0 minutes.
Serves: 2

Ingredients:

- 1/2 avocado, peeled and cubed
- 1/3 cucumber
- 2 cups spinach
- 6 ounces coconut milk
- 6 ounces almond milk
- 1 teaspoon matcha powder
- 1/2 lime juice
- 1/2 scoop vanilla protein powder
- 1/2 teaspoon chia seeds

Preparation:

1. Blend avocado flesh with cucumber and the rest of the ingredients in a blender until smooth.
2. Serve.

Serving Suggestion: Enjoy this smoothie with breakfast muffins.

Variation Tip: Add some strawberries to the smoothie.

Nutritional Information Per Serving:
Calories 297 | Fat 15g |Sodium 202mg | Carbs 58.5g | Fiber 4g | Sugar 1g | Protein 7.3g

Egg Cups

Prep Time: 10 minutes.
Cook Time: 13 minutes.
Serves: 4

Ingredients:

- 4 eggs
- 8 egg whites
- ¼ c chopped green chilies
- 1 bunch green onions chopped
- 12 pieces of Canadian bacon
- 1 cup ripped spinach
- 1/8 teaspoons salt
- ½ teaspoons black pepper

Preparation:

1. Beat eggs with egg whites, green chilies, green onions, spinach, black pepper and salt in a bowl.
2. Place a bacon slice in each muffin cup of a muffin tray and press it.
3. Divide the egg mixture into the bacon cup.
4. Bake for 13 minutes in the oven at 350 degrees F.
5. Serve warm.

Serving Suggestion: Serve these cups with a green smoothie.

Variation Tip: Add sautéed ground chicken to the egg filling.

Nutritional Information Per Serving:
Calories 163 | Fat 6.5g |Sodium 548mg | Carbs 3.4g | Fiber 2g | Sugar 1g | Protein 22g

Sweet Potato Rounds

Prep Time: 15 minutes.
Cook Time: 22 minutes.
Serves: 6

Ingredients:

- 2 lbs. sweet potatoes
- 1 ½ tablespoons olive oil
- 1 teaspoon garlic powder
- 1 teaspoon chili powder
- 1 teaspoon salt
- Hot sauce
- Monterrey Jack and cheddar cheese, shredded
- 3 green onions
- Sour cream

Preparation:

1. At 450 degrees F, preheat your oven.
2. Slice the sweet potatoes into ¼ inch thick slices.
3. Toss the slices with 1 teaspoon salt, 1 teaspoon chili powder, 1 teaspoon garlic powder and 1 ½ tablespoon olive oil in a large bowl.
4. Spread these slices in a baking sheet, lined with parchment paper.
5. Bake the sweet potato slices for 10 minutes, flip and bake again for 10 minutes.
6. Top each potato slice with green onions, a dot of hot sauce, and shredded cheese.
7. Bake the potatoes for 2 minutes until the cheese is melted.
8. Garnish with sour cream and serve warm.

Serving Suggestion: Serve these rounds with tomato ketchup or cheese dip.

Variation Tip: Drizzle cinnamon ground on top.

Nutritional Information Per Serving:
Calories 148 | Fat 22g |Sodium 350mg | Carbs 32.2g | Fiber 0.7g | Sugar 1g | Protein 4.3g

Zucchini Bites

Prep Time: 15 minutes.
Cook Time: 10 minutes.
Serves: 6

Ingredients:

- 2 large zucchinis
- ½ cup pizza sauce
- 1 teaspoon oregano
- 2 cups mozzarella cheese
- ¼ cup parmesan cheese

Preparation:

1. At 450 degrees F, preheat your oven. Layer a baking sheet with a foil sheet.
2. Cut the zucchini into ¼ inch thick slice and place them on the baking sheet.
3. Top each slice with pizza sauce, oregano, and cheese.
4. Bake the zucchini slices for 5-10 minutes until the cheese is melted.
5. Serve warm.

Serving Suggestion: Serve the bites with cheese or yogurt dip.

Variation Tip: Drizzle black pepper ground on top before baking.

Nutritional Information Per Serving:
Calories 145 | Fat 9g |Sodium 48mg | Carbs 4g | Fiber 1g | Sugar 2g | Protein 10g

Cauliflower Bites

Prep Time: 15 minutes.
Cook Time: 20 minutes.
Serves: 8

Ingredients:

- 8 cups cauliflower florets
- 2 tablespoons olive oil
- ¼ teaspoon kosher salt
- 2 tablespoons hot sauce
- 1-2 tablespoons Sriracha
- 1 tablespoon butter, melted
- 1 tablespoon lemon juice

Preparation:

1. At 450 degrees F, preheat your oven.
2. Layer a rimmed baking sheet with cooking spray.
3. Toss cauliflower with salt and oil in a large bowl and spread evenly on the baking sheet.
4. Roast the cauliflower florets for 15 minutes in the preheated oven.
5. Mix hot sauce, lemon juice, butter and sriracha in a large bowl.
6. Toss in cauliflower and mix well to coat.
7. Return the cauliflower to the baking sheet and bake for 5 minutes.
8. Serve warm.

Serving Suggestion: Serve the cauliflower bites with tomato sauce.

Variation Tip: Coat the cauliflower with breadcrumbs before cooking.

Nutritional Information Per Serving:
Calories 104 | Fat 3g |Sodium 216mg | Carbs 17g | Fiber 3g | Sugar 4g | Protein 1g

Pancetta Wrapped Prunes

Prep Time: 15 minutes.
Cook Time: 11 minutes.
Serves: 8

Ingredients:

- 16 prunes, pitted
- 150g of Gorgonzola
- 16 pancetta slices
- 3 tablespoons vegetable oil
- 3 tablespoons of walnuts
- 1 handful of celery leaves
- Black pepper, to taste

Preparation:

1. Add prunes with water to a cooking pot, cover and boil for 5 minutes then drain.
2. Pat dry the prunes, and remove their pits.
3. Dice the gorgonzola into 16 cubes and insert one cube into each pitted prune.
4. Wrap each prune with a pancetta slice and insert a toothpick to secure it.

5. Set a pan with cooking oil over medium heat and sear the wrapped prunes for 2-3 minutes per side.
6. Garnish with walnuts, black pepper and celery leaves.
7. Enjoy.

Serving Suggestion: Serve the rolls with mayonnaise dip.

Variation Tip: Drizzle shredded coconut on top before serving.

Nutritional Information Per Serving:
Calories 180 | Fat 9g |Sodium 318mg | Carbs 19g | Fiber 5g | Sugar 3g | Protein 7g

Turkey Lettuce Wraps

Prep Time: 15 minutes.
Cook Time: 8 minutes.
Serves: 6

Ingredients:

- 1 lb. lean ground turkey
- 1 tablespoon vegetable oil
- 1 small onion, diced
- 2 garlic cloves, minced
- 1 teaspoon ginger, grated
- 1 bell pepper, diced
- 1 tablespoon soy sauce
- 2 tablespoons Hoisin
- 1 teaspoon sesame oil
- 2 teaspoons rice vinegar
- 2 green onions, minced
- Salt, to taste
- Black pepper, to taste
- Fresh lettuce leaves

Preparation:

1. Sauté onion with ginger, garlic and cooking oil in a large pan until soft.
2. Stir in turkey ground and sauté for 3 minutes.
3. Add rice vinegar, sesame oil, hoisin and soy sauce then mix well.
4. Stir in green onion and bell peppers then sauté for 5 minutes.
5. Adjust seasoning with black pepper and salt.
6. Divide this filling into the lettuce leaves.
7. Serve.

Serving Suggestion: Serve the wraps with cream cheese dip on the side.

Variation Tip: Toss turkey meat with shredded parmesan before cooking.

Nutritional Information Per Serving:
Calories 173 | Fat 8g |Sodium 146mg | Carbs 18g | Fiber 5g | Sugar 1g | Protein 7g

Bell Pepper Bites

Prep Time: 15 minutes.
Cook Time: 4 minutes.
Serves: 9

Ingredients:

- 1 medium green bell pepper
- 1 medium red bell pepper
- 1/4 cup almonds, sliced

- 4 ounces low-fat cream cheese
- 1 teaspoon lemon pepper seasoning blend
- 1 teaspoon lemon juice

Preparation:

1. Slice the peppers in half, lengthwise.
2. Destem and deseed the peppers and cut each half into 6 more pieces.
3. Roast almonds in a skillet for 4 minutes then grind in a food processor.
4. Mix cream cheese with lemon juice and lemon pepper in a mixing bowl for 2 minutes.
5. Stir in the almond ground and mix for 10 seconds.
6. Add this filling to the piping bag and pipe this mixture into the bell pepper piece.
7. Serve.

Serving Suggestion: Serve the peppers with chilli sauce or mayo dip.

Variation Tip: Add shredded cheese to the filling.

Nutritional Information Per Serving:
Calories 140 | Fat 5g |Sodium 244mg | Carbs 16g | Fiber 1g | Sugar 1g | Protein 17g

Avocado Shrimp Cucumber

Prep Time: 15 minutes.
Cook Time: 6 minutes.
Serves: 4

Ingredients:

- 1 cucumber, sliced into 1/2-inch slices
- 2 large avocados, halved and pitted
- Salt and black pepper to taste
- 2 teaspoons lemon juice

Marinade:

- 2 lbs. shrimp, peeled and deveined
- 2 garlic cloves, minced
- 1 1/2 teaspoon salt
- 1/2 teaspoon cayenne pepper
- 1 teaspoon paprika
- 3 tablespoons olive oil
- 1 tablespoon lemon juice

Preparation:

1. Mix shrimp with garlic, salt, cayenne pepper, paprika, olive oil and lemon juice.
2. Cover and leave this marinade for 30 minutes.
3. Mash avocado with black pepper and salt in a bowl.
4. At medium-high heat, preheat your grill.
5. Grill the shrimp in the grill for 3 minutes per side.
6. Set the cucumber slices on the serving platter.
7. Top these slices with avocado mash and place a grilled shrimp on top.
8. Enjoy.

Serving Suggestion: Serve the bites with spinach or cream cheese dip.

Variation Tip: Add shredded parmesan on top.

Nutritional Information Per Serving:
Calories 82 | Fat 4g |Sodium 232mg | Carbs 7g | Fiber 1g | Sugar 0g | Protein 4g

Queso Dip

Prep Time: 15 minutes.
Cook Time: 12 minutes.
Serves: 8

Ingredients:

- 1 lb. lean ground turkey
- 1 small onion diced
- 1 package. taco seasoning
- 2 tablespoons butter
- 2 ½ tablespoons flour
- 1 ½ cup milk
- 1/2 teaspoon salt
- 1/8 teaspoons black pepper
- 4 ounces sharp cheddar shredded
- 4 ounces can jalapeños drained, diced

Preparation:

1. Sauté turkey with onion in a large skillet until golden.
2. Add taco seasoning then mix well.
3. Sauté flour with butter in another pan for 2 minutes.
4. Remove it from the heat, pour in the milk and mix well until lump-free.
5. Add cheddar cheese, black pepper and salt then mix well until melted.
6. Stir in turkey meat mixture and diced jalapenos.
7. Serve warm.

Serving Suggestion: Serve the dip with zucchini fries.

Variation Tip: Add olive slices or tomato salad on top.

Nutritional Information Per Serving:
Calories 229 | Fat 5g |Sodium 510mg | Carbs 37g | Fiber 5g | Sugar 4g | Protein 11g

Peanut Butter Cookies

Prep Time: 15 minutes.
Cook Time: 12 minutes.
Serves: 4

Ingredients:

- 4 sachets optavia silky peanut butter shake
- 1/4 teaspoon baking powder
- 1/4 cup unsweetened almond milk
- 1 tablespoon butter, melted
- 1/4 teaspoon vanilla extract
- 1/8 teaspoon salt

Preparation:

1. At 350 degrees F, preheat your oven.
2. Mix baking powder with peanut butter fueling in a bowl.
3. Stir in vanilla extract, melted butter, and almond milk, then mix until smooth.
4. Divide the dough into 8 cookies and place in a baking sheet, lined with parchment paper.
5. Flatten the cookies and bake for 12 minutes in the preheated oven.
6. Allow the cookies to cool and serve.

Serving Suggestion: Serve the cookies with pure maple or apple sauce.

Variation Tip: Drizzle maple syrup on top before serving.

Nutritional Information Per Serving:
Calories 201 | Fat 7g |Sodium 269mg | Carbs 35g | Fiber 4g | Sugar 12g | Protein 6g

Goat Cheese Crostini

Prep Time: 15 minutes.
Cook Time: 10 minutes.
Serves: 2

Ingredients:

- 1 baguette
- 4-ounce goat cheese
- Honey
- Fresh mint, chopped
- Ground black pepper

Preparation:

1. At 350 degrees F, preheat your oven.
2. Cut the baguette into thin slices, diagonally.
3. Place the baguette slices in a baking sheet and bake for 10 minutes.
4. Divide goat cheese, honey, herbs, and black pepper on top of the bread slices.
5. Enjoy.

Serving Suggestion: Serve the crostini with chilli garlic sauce.

Variation Tip: Add sliced olives to the topping.

Nutritional Information Per Serving:
Calories 348 | Fat 12g |Sodium 710mg | Carbs 44g | Fiber 5g | Sugar 3g | Protein 11g

Buffalo Cauliflower

Prep Time: 15 minutes.
Cook Time: 36 minutes.
Serves: 4

Ingredients:

Buffalo cauliflower

- 1 head cauliflower
- 2 tablespoons olive oil
- ½ teaspoon kosher salt

Buffalo sauce

- 2 tablespoons unsalted butter
- 1 garlic clove
- ¼ cup Frank's hot sauce

Blue cheese sauce

- 1 cup plain yogurt
- ½ cup blue cheese crumbles
- 1/4 teaspoon salt
- 1 teaspoon garlic powder
- Fresh ground black pepper
- Celery, to serve

Preparation:

1. At 450 degrees F, preheat your oven.
2. Cut the cauliflower head into small florets and toss them with salt and olive oil on a baking sheet.
3. Bake the cauliflower for 35 minutes in the preheated oven.
4. For buffalo sauce, sauté garlic with butter in a saucepan for 30 seconds.
5. Stir in hot sauce and sauté for 30 seconds.
6. Toss in the cauliflower florets and mix well with the sauce.
7. For cheese dip, blend all its ingredients in a blender.
8. Serve the cauliflower with cream cheese dip.
9. Enjoy.

Serving Suggestion: Serve the florets with tomato ketchup.

Variation Tip: Coat the cauliflower in breadcrumbs before cooking.

Nutritional Information Per Serving:
Calories 175 | Fat 16g | Sodium 255mg | Carbs 31g | Fiber 1.2g | Sugar 5g | Protein 4.1g

Peanut Butter Brownie

Prep Time: 15 minutes.
Cook Time: 1 minute.
Serves: 4

Ingredients:

- 3 tablespoons peanut butter powder
- 3 tablespoons water
- 6 packets optavia double chocolate brownie fueling
- 1 cup of water

Preparation:

1. Mix peanut butter powder with water and chocolate brownie in a bowl.
2. Divide this batter on a baking sheet lined with parchment paper into small mounds.
3. Cover and freeze for 40 minutes.
4. Serve.

Serving Suggestion: Serve the brownies with chocolate dip.

Variation Tip: Dip the brownies in white chocolate syrup.

Nutritional Information Per Serving:
Calories 361 | Fat 10g | Sodium 218mg | Carbs 56g | Fiber 10g | Sugar 30g | Protein 14g

Chocolate Cherry Cookie

Prep Time: 15 minutes.
Cook Time: 12 minutes.
Serves: 4

Ingredients:

- 1 Optavia dark chocolate covered cherry shake
- ½ teaspoons baking powder
- 2 tablespoons water

Preparation:

1. At 350 degrees F, preheat your oven.
2. Mix cherry shake with water and baking powder in a bowl.
3. Divide this batter on a baking sheet, lined with parchment paper, into 8 small cookies.

4. Bake these cookies 12 minutes in the preheated oven.
5. Serve.

Serving Suggestion: Serve the cookies with fresh berries on top.

Variation Tip: Add cherry preserves at the centre of the cookies.

Nutritional Information Per Serving:
Calories 118 | Fat 20g |Sodium 192mg | Carbs 23.7g | Fiber 0.9g | Sugar 19g | Protein 5.2g

Stuffed pears with almonds

Prep Time: 15 minutes.
Cook Time: 25 minutes.
Serves: 6
Ingredients:

Spices

- 4 pinches cinnamon
- 3 ounces flour
- 3 ounces granulated sugar
- 2 tablespoons soup brown sugar
- 3 ounces almonds, powdered
- 1 ½ ounces frilled almond
- 1 ½ ounces hazelnut
- 3 ½ ounces butter
- 6 pears

Preparation:

1. Mix butter with cinnamon, sugars, flour, almonds, hazelnut in a food processor.
2. Core the pears and divide the nuts mixture into these pears.
3. Place the stuffed pears on a baking sheet.
4. Bake these pears for 25 minutes in the oven at 300 degrees F.
5. Serve once cooled.

Serving Suggestion: Serve the pears with a scoop of vanilla cream on top.

Variation Tip: Add chopped pecans to the filling as well.

Nutritional Information Per Serving:
Calories 248 | Fat 16g |Sodium 95mg | Carbs 38.4g | Fiber 0.3g | Sugar 10g | Protein 14.1g

Peanut Butter Cups

Prep Time: 15 minutes.
Cook Time: 12 minutes.
Serves: 4
Ingredients:

- 1/4 cup creamy peanut butter
- 5 ounces chocolate
- Cacao Nibs, Sea Salt

Preparation:

1. Melt chocolate with peanut butter in a bowl by heating it in the microwave.
2. Mix well and divide this mixture into 12 mini muffin cups.
3. Cover and refrigerate for 1 hour.

4. Serve.

Serving Suggestion: Serve the cups with chocolate or apple sauce.

Variation Tip: Dip the bites in white chocolate syrup.

Nutritional Information Per Serving:
Calories 117 | Fat 12g |Sodium 79mg | Carbs 24.8g | Fiber 1.1g | Sugar 18g | Protein 5g

Medifast Rolls

Prep Time: 15 minutes.
Cook Time: 35 minutes.
Serves: 4

Ingredients:

- 3 eggs, separated
- 3 tablespoons cream cheese
- Pinch cream of tartar
- 1 packet Splenda

Preparation:

1. At 350 degrees F, preheat your oven.
2. Beat separated egg whites with cream of tartar in a bowl until fluffy.
3. Blend yolks with Splenda and cream cheese in a bowl until pale.
4. Fold in egg whites and mix gently.
5. Layer a baking sheet with parchment paper.
6. Divide the batter onto the baking sheet into cookie rounds.
7. Bake these rolls for 35 minutes in the oven at 350 degrees F.
8. Serve once cooled.

Serving Suggestion: Serve the rolls with creamy frosting on top.

Variation Tip: Add chopped pecans or walnuts to the batter.

Nutritional Information Per Serving:
Calories 195 | Fat 3g |Sodium 355mg | Carbs 20g | Fiber 1g | Sugar 25g | Protein 1g

Apple Crisp

Prep Time: 15 minutes.
Cook Time: 40 minutes.
Serves: 4

Ingredients:

- 4 cups apples, peeled and sliced
- 1 tablespoon coconut oil, melted
- 1/2 teaspoon cinnamon
- 1/4 teaspoon ground ginger

Crisp Topping

- ½ teaspoon cinnamon
- ¼ teaspoon ginger
- ¼ teaspoon nutmeg
- 1 cup old fashioned oats
- 1/3 cup pecans chopped
- 2 tablespoons coconut oil
- 1 tablespoon maple syrup

Preparation:

1. At 350 degrees F, preheat your oven. Grease an 8x8 inch baking dish.
2. Toss apples with coconut oil, ginger and cinnamon in a bowl.
3. Spread the apples in the baking dish.
4. Mix all the crisp topping in a bowl and drizzle over the apples.
5. Cover this baking dish with aluminium foil and bake for 20 minutes at 350 degrees F.
6. Uncover the hot dish and bake for another 20 minutes.
7. Serve.

Serving Suggestion: Serve the apple crisp with chopped nuts on top.

Variation Tip: Add dried raisins to the apple crisp.

Nutritional Information Per Serving:
Calories 203 | Fat 8.9g |Sodium 340mg | Carbs 24.7g | Fiber 1.2g | Sugar 11.3g | Protein 5.3g

Cherry Dessert

Prep Time: 15 minutes.
Cook Time: 0 minutes.
Serves: 4

Ingredients:

- 2 cups lite whipped topping, thawed
- 1 (8-ounce) package cream cheese, softened
- 1 package sugar-free cherry gelatin
- 1/2 cup boiling water

Preparation:

1. Beat cream with cream cheese in a bowl until smooth.
2. Mix gelatin mix with boiling water in a bowl.
3. Add this prepared gelatin mixture to the cream cheese mixture.
4. Mix well and spread this mixture into a pie pan.
5. Cover and refrigerate the cream cheese for 2 hours.
6. Serve.

Serving Suggestion: Serve the cherry dessert with fresh berries on top.

Variation Tip: Add vanilla extracts to the dessert.

Nutritional Information Per Serving:
Calories 153 | Fat 1g |Sodium 8mg | Carbs 66g | Fiber 0.8g | Sugar 56g | Protein 1g

Vanilla Pudding

Prep Time: 15 minutes.
Cook Time: 8 minutes.
Serves: 4

Ingredients:

- 2 cups of milk
- 1/4 teaspoon salt
- 1/2 cup milk
- 3 tablespoons cornstarch
- 3/4 teaspoons pure vanilla extract
- 1/8 teaspoons stevia
- 2 teaspoons buttery spread

Preparation:

1. Warm 2 cup milk in a saucepan.

2. Mix cornstarch with ½ cup milk in a bowl and pour into the saucepan.
3. Cook this milk mixture for 3 minutes until it thickens,
4. Stir in remaining ingredients, then mix well.
5. Allow this pudding to cool and serve.

Serving Suggestion: Serve the pudding with chocolate syrup or berries on top.

Variation Tip: Add crushed walnuts or pecans to the custard.

Nutritional Information Per Serving:
Calories 198 | Fat 14g |Sodium 272mg | Carbs 34g | Fiber 1g | Sugar 9.3g | Protein 1.3g

Banana Cookies

Prep Time: 10 minutes.
Cook Time: 15 minutes.
Serves: 4

Ingredients:

- 2 ripe bananas
- 1/3 cup almond milk
- 1 cup all-purpose flour
- 1/2 teaspoon baking powder

Preparation:

1. At 350 degrees F, preheat your oven.
2. Mash bananas with almond milk in a mixing bowl.
3. Stir in baking powder and flour, then mix well.
4. Divide the batter into 13 cookies using a scoop onto a baking sheet with parchment paper.
5. Bake these cookies for 15 minutes in the oven.
6. Allow the cookies to cool.
7. Serve.

Serving Suggestion: Serve the cookies with chocolate sauce.

Variation Tip: Roll the cookies in crushed nuts or coconut flakes before cooking.

Nutritional Information Per Serving:
Calories 159 | Fat 3g |Sodium 277mg | Carbs 21g | Fiber 1g | Sugar 9g | Protein 2g

Sweet Potato Cheesecake

Prep Time: 10 minutes.
Cook Time: 15 minutes.
Serves: 6

Ingredients:

- 1 egg, whole
- ¼ cup yogurt cheese
- 1/2 cup coconut milk
- 1/8 teaspoons pumpkin pie spice
- ½ teaspoons vanilla
- 1 tablespoon maple syrup
- 2 package optavia honey sweet potatoes
- ½ teaspoons sweet leaf stevia powdered

To garnish:

- 15 almonds, chopped

Preparation:

1. Blend honey sweet potato fueling with the rest of the ingredients in a bowl.
2. Divide this mixture into 6 muffin cups and drizzle almond on top.
3. Bake for 15 in the oven at 350 degrees F.
4. Serve.

Serving Suggestion: Serve the cakes with cream frosting on top.

Variation Tip: Add chocolate chips or a teaspoon of crushed nuts to the batter for the change of flavor.

Nutritional Information Per Serving:

Calories 245 | Fat 14g |Sodium 122mg | Carbs 23.3g | Fiber 1.2g | Sugar 12g | Protein 4.3g

Cauliflower Breakfast Casserole

Prep Time: 10 minutes.
Cook Time: 55 minutes.
Serves: 8

Ingredients:

- 8 ounces turkey sausage, cooked
- ¼ cup onion, chopped
- 2 cups cauliflower florets
- ½ teaspoon Jalapeno Seasoning
- ¼ teaspoon salt
- ¼ teaspoon black pepper
- 6 turkey bacon slices, cooked and chopped
- 2 cups Mexican cheese, shredded
- 8 large eggs
- 16 ounces egg whites
- ¼ cup almond milk

Preparation:

1. At 350 degrees F, preheat your oven.
2. Grease a baking dish with cooking spray.
3. Saute turkey sausage in a skillet until golden brown.
4. Saute onions and cauliflower in a same skillet until golden.
5. Stir in black pepper, salt, jalapeno seasoning then mix well.
6. Sread the cauliflower mixture in the prepared baking dish.
7. Top this mixture with cheese and bacon.
8. Beat egg whites with eggs and almond milk in a bowl.
9. Pour this mixture over the turkey mixture.
10. Bake for 45 minutes in the oven.
11. Garnish with green onions.
12. Serve warm.

Serving Suggestion: Enjoy this breakfast casserole with a refreshing smoothie.

Variation Tip: Add some chopped or shredded zucchini to the casserole.

Nutritional Information Per Serving:

Calories 244 | Fat 7.9g |Sodium 704mg | Carbs 19g | Fiber 2g | Sugar 14g | Protein 14g

Quinoa Pudding

Prep Time: 10 minutes.
Cook Time: 25 minutes.
Serves: 4

Ingredients:

- 1 cup quinoa
- 4 cups coconut milk
- 1/3 cup maple syrup
- 1 ½ teaspoons vanilla extract
- 1 teaspoon cinnamon
- 1/4 teaspoon salt

Preparation:

1. Mix quinoa, milk, maple, vanilla, cinnamon and salt in a saucepan.
2. Boil this mixture, reduce the heat and cook for 25 minutes.
3. Garnish with your favorite toppings.
4. Serve warm.

Serving Suggestion: Serve this pudding with toasted bread slices.

Variation Tip: Add chopped berries and nuts to the pudding.

Nutritional Information Per Serving:
Calories 214 | Fat 5.1g |Sodium 231mg | Carbs 31g | Fiber 5g | Sugar 2.1g | Protein 7g

Cranberry Sweet Potato Muffins

Prep Time: 15 minutes.
Cook Time: 20 minutes.
Serves: 4

Ingredients:

- 2 tablespoons butter, melted
- 1/4 cup brown sugar
- 1 egg
- 1 teaspoon vanilla
- 1/4 cup skim milk
- 1/2 cup curd cottage cheese
- 1/2 cup cooked sweet potato, mashed
- 3/4 cup white whole wheat flour
- 1 teaspoon baking powder
- 1 cup fresh cranberries

Preparation:

1. Mix all the ingredients for batter in a bowl until smooth.
2. Stir in cranberries then divide the batter into muffin cups.
3. Bake for 20 minutes at 350 degrees F.
4. Allow the cranberries to cool then serve.

Serving Suggestion: Enjoy these muffins with a refreshing smoothie.

Variation Tip: Add some riasins to the muffins.

Nutritional Information Per Serving:
Calories 225 | Fat 9g |Sodium 118mg | Carbs 35.4g | Fiber 2.9g | Sugar 15g | Protein 6.5g

Quinoa Bars

Prep Time: 15 minutes.
Cook Time: 20 minutes.
Serves: 6

Ingredients:

- 1 cup whole wheat flour
- 1 ½ cup cooked quinoa
- 2 cup oats
- 1/2 cup nuts, chopped
- 1 teaspoon cinnamon
- 1 teaspoon baking soda
- 2 tablespoons chia seeds
- 2/3 cup peanut butter
- 1/2 cup honey
- 2 eggs
- 2/3 cup applesauce
- 1teaspoons vanilla
- 1/2 teaspoon salt
- 1/3 cup craisins
- 1/3 cup chocolate chips

Preparation:

1. Mix quinoa with honey, peanut butter, eggs, vanilla, applesauce in a small bowl.
2. Stir in rest of the ingredients then mix well.
3. Spread this mixture in a 9x13 greased baking dish.
4. Bake for 20 minutes at 375 degrees F then cut into bars.
5. Serve.

Serving Suggestion: Enjoy these bars with a strawberry smoothie.

Variation Tip: Add some goji berries to the bars.

Nutritional Information Per Serving:

Calories 163 | Fat 2.5g |Sodium 15.6mg | Carbs 49.5g | Fiber 7.6g | Sugar 28g | Protein 3.5g

Buckwheat Crepes

Prep Time: 15 minutes.
Cook Time: 10 minutes.
Serves: 4

Ingredients:

- 2/3 cup buckwheat flour
- 1/3 cup whole wheat flour
- 2 eggs
- 1 ¼ cup skim milk
- 1 tablespoon honey
- Fruit and Greek yogurt, for filling

Preparation:

1. Mix flours with eggs, milk, and honey in a bowl until smooth.
2. Set a nonstick skillet over medium heat.
3. Add a ¼ cup batter into the skillet, spread it evenly then cook for 2 minutes per side.

4. Transfer the crepe to a plate and then cook the remaining batter in the same way.
5. Garnish with fruits and yogurt.
6. Serve.

Serving Suggestion: Enjoy these crepes with a blueberry smoothie.

Variation Tip: Add some blueberries to the crepes filling.

Nutritional Information Per Serving:
Calories 112 | Fat 25g |Sodium 132mg | Carbs 44g | Fiber 3.9g | Sugar 3g | Protein 8.9g

Oatmeal Pancakes

Prep Time: 10 minutes.
Cook Time: 10 minutes.
Serves: 6

Ingredients:

- 2/3 cup Greek Yogurt
- 3 tablespoons skim milk
- 1 tablespoon applesauce
- 1 egg
- 1/2 cup white whole wheat flour
- 3/4 cup oats, crushed
- 1 teaspoon baking powder
- 1/2 teaspoon baking soda
- 1 tablespoon ground flaxseed
- 1 teaspoon cinnamon

Preparation:

1. Mix flours and rest of the ingredients in a bowl until smooth.
2. Set a hot griddle over medium heat.
3. Pour a ladle of battter over the griddle and cook the pancake for 2 mintues per side.
4. Transfer to a plate and cook remaining pancakes in the same manner.
5. Serve warm.

Serving Suggestion: Enjoy these pancakes with a spinach smoothie.

Variation Tip: Add chopped nuts to the batter.

Nutritional Information Per Serving:
Calories 190 | Fat 15g |Sodium 595mg | Carbs 11g | Fiber 3g | Sugar 12g | Protein 9g

Blueberry Muffins

Prep Time: 15 minutes.
Cook Time: 30 minutes.
Serves: 4

Ingredients:

- 2 tablespoons butter, melted
- 1 cup fresh blueberries
- 1/4 cup sugar
- 1 egg
- 1 teaspoon vanilla
- 1/4 cup skim milk
- 1/2 cup curd cottage cheese

- 1/2 cup cooked sweet potato, mashed
- 3/4 cup whole wheat flour
- 1 teaspoon baking powder

Preparation:

1. Mix sweet potato mash with all the ingredients except cranberries in a bowl until smooth.
2. Fold in blueberries then mix evenly.
3. Divide the batter into the muffin tray and bake for 30 minutes at 350 degrees F.
4. Serve.

Serving Suggestion: Enjoy these muffins with a strawberry smoothie.

Variation Tip: Add raisins to the muffin batter.

Nutritional Information Per Serving:

Calories 197 | Fat 15g |Sodium 202mg | Carbs 58.5g | Fiber 4g | Sugar 1g | Protein 7.3g

Berry Quinoa

Prep Time: 10 minutes.
Cook Time: 20 minutes.
Serves: 4

Ingredients:

- ¼ cup quinoa, rinsed
- 1/2 cup almond milk
- 1/2 cup berries
- 1 dash cinnamon
- 1/2 teaspoon vanilla

Toppings

- Nuts
- Fruit
- Chocolate chips
- Nut butter
- Agave/honey

Preparation:

1. Mix quinoa with milk, vanilla, cinnamon and berries in a saucepan.
2. Cook to a boil, reduce its heat and cook for 20 minutes until liquid is absorved.
3. Garnish with desired toppings.
4. Serve.

Serving Suggestion: Enjoy this quinoa with a cranberry muffin.

Variation Tip: Add roasted nuts to the quinoa.

Nutritional Information Per Serving:

Calories 163 | Fat 6.5g |Sodium 548mg | Carbs 3.4g | Fiber 2g | Sugar 1g | Protein 2g

Celery Salad

Prep Time: 5 minutes.
Cook Time: 0 minutes.
Serves: 2

Ingredients:

- 1 cup celery, chopped
- 1 tablespoon mint, chopped
- 1 teaspoon lemon juice
- 1 teaspoon olive oil

Preparation:

1. Mix celery with mint, lemon juice and olive oil in a salad bowl.
2. Serve.

Serving Suggestion: Serve this salad with grilled shrimp.

Variation Tip: Drizzle dried herbs and cumin on top.

Nutritional Information Per Serving:
Calories 148 | Fat 22g |Sodium 350mg | Carbs 32.2g | Fiber 0.7g | Sugar 1g | Protein 4.3g

Taco Salad

Prep Time: 5 minutes.
Cook Time: 0 minutes.
Serves: 2

Ingredients:

- 5 ounces ground turkey
- 1 tablespoon taco seasoning
- 2 tablespoons salsa
- 1 cup romaine lettuce
- 1 cup iceberg lettuce
- 1/2 cup diced tomatoes
- 1 tablespoon water

Preparation:

1. Saute turkey with taco seasoning in a skillet until golden brown.
2. Transfer to a salad bowl and stir in salsa, lettuces, tomatoes and water.
3. Mix well and serve.

Serving Suggestion: Serve this salad with grilled chicken.

Variation Tip: Drizzle black pepper ground on top before serving.

Nutritional Information Per Serving:
Calories 345 | Fat 9g |Sodium 48mg | Carbs 14g | Fiber 1g | Sugar 2g | Protein 20g

Yogurt Trail Mix Bars

Prep Time: 15 minutes.
Cook Time: 0 minutes.
Serves: 4

Ingredients:

- 2 cups Greek yogurt
- 1 ½ cups fruit
- 1/2 cup almonds, chopped
- 3/4 cup granola
- 1/4 cup chocolate chips

Preparation:

1. Mix yogurt with fruit, almonds, granola and chocolate chips in a bowl.
2. Spread this mixture in a shallow tray and freeze for 1 hour.
3. Cut the mixture into bars.
4. Serve.

Serving Suggestion: Serve these bars with a berry compote.

Variation Tip: Pour melted chocolates on top and then slice to serve.

Nutritional Information Per Serving:

Calories 204 | Fat 3g |Sodium 216mg | Carbs 17g | Fiber 3g | Sugar 4g | Protein 11g

Curried Tuna Salad

Prep Time: 15 minutes.
Cook Time: 0 minutes.
Serves: 2

Ingredients:

- 2 cans of tuna, drained
- ¼ cup hummus
- ¼ cup avocado, smashed
- ½ cup apple, chopped
- ¼ cup onion, diced
- 1 tablespoon lemon juice
- 2 teaspoons curry powder
- 1/2 teaspoon dry mustard powder

Preparation:

1. Mix tuna with rest of the ingredients in a salad bowl.
2. Serve fresh.

Serving Suggestion: Serve this salad with grilled shrimp.

Variation Tip: Drizzle shredded coconut on top before serving.

Nutritional Information Per Serving:

Calories 280 | Fat 9g |Sodium 318mg | Carbs 19g | Fiber 5g | Sugar 3g | Protein 17g

Tuna Quinoa Cakes

Prep Time: 15 minutes.
Cook Time: 20 minutes.
Serves: 4

Ingredients:

- 1/2 cup cooked sweet potato, mashed
- 2 cans tuna, drained
- 3/4 cup cooked quinoa
- 1/4 cup green onion, chopped
- 2 garlic cloves, minced
- 1 tablespoon lemon juice
- 1 egg
- 1/4 cup plain yogurt
- 1 tablespoon mustard
- 1/2 teaspoon cayenne pepper
- 1 teaspoon paprika
- 1/2 cup breadcrumbs

Preparation:

1. In a small bowl, combine the tuna and sweet potato and mix well.
2. Add remaining ingredients and stir until well combined.
3. Make 6 patties out of this mixture.
4. Place the patties in a greased baking sheet and bake for 20 minutes at 400 degrees F.
5. Flip the patties once cooked half way through.
6. Serve warm.

Serving Suggestion: Serve the cakes with cream cheese dip on the side.

Variation Tip: Add shredded parmesan before cooking.

Nutritional Information Per Serving:
Calories 273 | Fat 8g |Sodium 146mg | Carbs 18g | Fiber 5g | Sugar 1g | Protein 7g

Taco Cups

Prep Time: 15 minutes.
Cook Time: 25 minutes.
Serves: 4

Ingredients:

- 2 Sargento cheese slices
- 4 ounces lean ground beef
- 1 teaspoon taco seasoning

Toppings:

- Lettuce and tomatoes
- 1 tablespoon sour cream

Preparation:

1. At 375 degrees F, preheat your oven.
2. Sauté beef in a skillet for 5 minutes.
3. Stir in taco seasoning then mix well.
4. Layer a baking sheet with wax paper.
5. Place cheese slices in the baking sheet and bake for 7 minutes in the oven.

6. Allow the cheese to cool and then place each cheese round in the muffin tray.
7. Press the cheese into cups and divide the beef into these cups.
8. Garnish with desired toppings.
9. Serve warm.

Serving Suggestion: Serve the cups with guacamole.

Variation Tip: Add shredded cheese to the filling.

Nutritional Information Per Serving:
Calories 240 | Fat 25g |Sodium 244mg | Carbs 16g | Fiber 1g | Sugar 1g | Protein 27g

Caprese Spaghetti Squash Nests

Prep Time: 15 minutes.
Cook Time: 1 hr 35 minutes.
Serves: 4

Ingredients:

For the Nests:

- 1 medium spaghetti squash
- 1/4 teaspoon salt
- 1/4 teaspoon black pepper
- 1/4 teaspoon garlic powder
- 3 tablespoons egg whites

Filling:

- 1 cup cherry tomatoes
- 1/4 teaspoon salt
- 1/4 teaspoon black pepper
- 4 ounces mozzarella cheese, shredded
- 1/4 cup basil, chopped

Preparation:

1. At 375 degrees F, preheat your oven.
2. Cut the spaghetti squash in half and place in the baking sheet.
3. Bake the squash for 45 minutes in the oven.
4. Scrape the squash with a fork and divide the shreds in the muffin tray.
5. Beat egg whites with garlic powder, black pepper and salt.
6. Divide this liquid mixture into the muffin cups, make a nest at the center of each and bake for 20 minutes.
7. Spread tomatoes in a baking sheet and bake for 20 minutes in the oven.
8. Divide the roasted tomaotes in the spaghetti squash and top them with cheese and rest of the ingredients.
9. Bake for 10 minutes in the oven.
10. Serve warm.

Serving Suggestion: Serve the nests with spinach or cream cheese dip.

Variation Tip: Add shredded parmesan on top.

Nutritional Information Per Serving:
Calories 282 | Fat 4g |Sodium 232mg | Carbs 7g | Fiber 1g | Sugar 0g | Protein 14g

Fire Cracker Shrimp

Prep Time: 15 minutes.
Cook Time: 6 minutes.
Serves: 4

Ingredients:

- 11 ounces raw shrimp, peeled
- 2 tablespoons Apricot Preserves
- 1 teaspoon lite soy sauce
- ½ teaspoon sriracha sauce
- 1 teaspoon sesame oil

Preparation:

1. Place apricot in a small bowl and heat for 20 seconds in the microwave.
2. Mix oil, sriracha sauce, soy sauce and apricot mixture in a bowl.
3. Thread the shrimp on the wooden skewers and brush them with apricot mixture.
4. Grill these skewers for 3 minutes per side.
5. Serve warm.

Serving Suggestion: Serve the shrimp with zucchini fries.

Variation Tip: Add crumbled cheese on top.

Nutritional Information Per Serving:
Calories 229 | Fat 5g |Sodium 510mg | Carbs 37g | Fiber 5g | Sugar 4g | Protein 21g

Crispy Zucchini Chips

Prep Time: 15 minutes.
Cook Time: 4 hrs.
Serves: 4

Ingredients:

- 1 ½ cups zucchini
- 1 teaspoon olive oil
- 1/8 teaspoons salt

Preparation:

1. At 200 degrees F, preheat your oven.
2. Layer a baking sheet with wax paper and grease with cooking spray.
3. Spread the zucchini slices in the baking sheet and bake for 4 hours.
4. Flip the zucchinin once cooked half way through.
5. Serve warm.

Serving Suggestion: Serve the chips with tomato sauce.

Variation Tip: Drizzle black pepper on top before serving.

Nutritional Information Per Serving:
Calories 101 | Fat 7g |Sodium 269mg | Carbs 5g | Fiber 4g | Sugar 12g | Protein 1g

Baked Kale Chips

Prep Time: 15 minutes.
Cook Time: 15 minutes.
Serves: 4

Ingredients:

- 4 ½ cups kale
- 1 tablespoon olive oil
- 1/4 teaspoon salt

Preparation:

1. At 450-degree F, preheat your oven.
2. Layer a baking sheet with parchment paper.
3. Toss the kale leaves with salt, and olive oil in the baking sheet.
4. Spread them evenly then bake for 15 minutes in the oven.
5. Serve.

Serving Suggestion: Serve these chips with chilli garlic sauce.

Variation Tip: Add some paprika or red pepper flakes to the topping.

Nutritional Information Per Serving:
Calories 118 | Fat 11g |Sodium 110mg | Carbs 4g | Fiber 5g | Sugar 3g | Protein 1g

Chia Seed Pudding

Prep Time: 15 minutes.
Cook Time: 0 minute.
Serves: 2

Ingredients:

- 2 cups almond milk
- 1/2 cup chia seeds
- 1/4 cup almond butter
- 1/4 cup cocoa powder unsweetened
- 4 dates large, pitted and chopped
- 1 teaspoon pure vanilla extract

Preparation:

1. Blend all the pudding ingredients in a bowl.
2. Cover and refrigerate this pudding for 4 hours.
3. Serve.

Serving Suggestion: Serve the pudding with goji berries on top.

Variation Tip: Add white chocolate syrup on top.

Nutritional Information Per Serving:
Calories 361 | Fat 10g |Sodium 218mg | Carbs 56g | Fiber 10g | Sugar 30g | Protein 4g

Grilled Buffalo Shrimp

Prep Time: 15 minutes.
Cook Time: 8 minutes.
Serves: 4

Ingredients:

- 11 ounce raw shrimp, peeled
- 1/4 cup Frank's Hot Sauce
- 1 tablespoon butter

Preparation:

1. Mix butter with hot sauce in a bowl.
2. Thread the shrimp on the skewers and brush them with butter mixture.
3. Grill these skewers for 2 minutes per side while basting with butter sauce.
4. Serve warm.

Serving Suggestion: Serve the shrimps with tomato ketchup.

Variation Tip: Coat the shrimp in breadcrumbs before cooking.

Nutritional Information Per Serving:

Calories 275 | Fat 16g |Sodium 255mg | Carbs 1g | Fiber 1.2g | Sugar 5g | Protein 19g

Strawberry Ice Cream

Prep Time: 10 minutes.
Cook Time: 0 minutes.
Serves: 6

Ingredients:

- 16 ounce strawberries, frozen
- 3/4 cup Greek yogurt plain
- 2 tablespoons balsamic vinegar
- 2 tablespoons honey

Preparation:

1. Blend all the ingredients for ice cream in a blender until smooth.
2. Divide the mixture in the ice-cream molds.
3. Freeze the ice cream for 4 hours.
4. Serve.

Serving Suggestion: Serve the ice cream with fresh berries on top.

Variation Tip: Add strawberry preserves on top of the ice cream.

Nutritional Information Per Serving:

Calories 118 | Fat 20g |Sodium 192mg | Carbs 23.7g | Fiber 0.9g | Sugar 19g | Protein 5.2g

Strawberry Yogurt

Prep Time: 5 minutes.
Cook Time: 0 minutes.
Serves: 2

Ingredients:

Spices

- 1 cup Greek yogurt plain
- 3/4 cup strawberry fruit spread

Preparation:

1. Blend yogurt with strawberries in a blender.
2. Serve.

Serving Suggestion: Serve the yogurt with berries on top.

Variation Tip: Add chopped pecans to the yogurt as well.

Nutritional Information Per Serving:

Calories 248 | Fat 16g |Sodium 95mg | Carbs 38.4g | Fiber 0.3g | Sugar 10g | Protein 14.1g

Banana Pops

Prep Time: 15 minutes.
Cook Time: 0 minutes.
Serves: 2

Ingredients:

- 3 bananas
- 3 tablespoons cacao powder raw
- 2 liquid stevia drops
- 3 ounces water
- 1/4 cup cacao nibs raw
- 1/4 cup goji berries raw

Preparation:

1. Insert a stick into each banana.
2. Place these bananas in the freezer for 30 minutes.
3. Mash the remaining banana with stevia, water and cacao powder in a bowl.
4. Dip the bananas on the stick in the cacao mmixture.
5. Coat them with cacao nibs and gji berries.
6. Serve.

Serving Suggestion: Serve the pops with chocolate or apple sauce.

Variation Tip: Dip the bananas in white chocolate syrup.

Nutritional Information Per Serving:

Calories 117 | Fat 12g |Sodium 79mg | Carbs 24.8g | Fiber 1.1g | Sugar 18g | Protein 5g

Strawberry Cheesecake

Prep Time: 15 minutes.
Cook Time: 0 minutes.
Serves: 6

Ingredients:

- 1/2 cup cream cheese
- 2 tablespoons coconut palm sugar
- 1/2 cup Greek yogurt
- 2 teaspoons lemon juice, squeezed
- 1/4 cup strawberry preserves
- 1 cup strawberries diced
- 1/3 cup almonds whole
- 4 dates

Preparation:

1. Beat cream cheese with lemon juice, yogurt, and sugar in a blender for 3 minutes.
2. Mix strawberries with preserves in a small bowl.
3. Grind the almonds with dates in a food processor.
4. Divide the almond mixture in a muffin tray and press it.
5. Add cheesecake batter on top and divide the strawberry mixture on top.
6. Refirgerate these mini cheese cakes for 1 hour.
7. Serve.

Serving Suggestion: Serve the cheese cakes with creamy frosting on top.

Variation Tip: Add chopped pecans or walnuts to the batter.

Nutritional Information Per Serving:

Calories 195 | Fat 3g |Sodium 355mg | Carbs 20g | Fiber 1g | Sugar 25g | Protein 1g

Coffee Cake Muffins

Prep Time: 15 minutes.
Cook Time: 15 minutes.
Serves: 4

Ingredients:

- 1 packet medifast cappuccino
- 1 packet medifast chocolate chip pancakes
- 1 packet of stevia
- 1 tablespoon egg, beaten
- 1/4 teaspoon baking powder
- 1/4 cup water

Preparation:

1. Mix cappuccino fueling and rest of the ingredients in a bowl until smooth.
2. Divide the mixture into the muffin tray.
3. Bake the muffins for 15 minutes in the oven at 350 degrees F.
4. Allow the muffins to cool and serve.

Serving Suggestion: Serve the muffins with chopped nuts on top.

Variation Tip: Add dried raisins to the muffins.

Nutritional Information Per Serving:

Calories 203 | Fat 8.9g |Sodium 340mg | Carbs 24.7g | Fiber 1.2g | Sugar 11.3g | Protein 5.3g

Peanut Butter Balls

Prep Time: 15 minutes.
Cook Time: 0 minutes.
Serves: 4

Ingredients:

- 1 Medifast chocolate pudding
- 1 Medifast chocolate shake
- 4 tablespoons powdered peanut butter
- 2 tablespoons water
- 1/4 cup unsweetened almond milk

Preparation:

1. Mix chocolate pudding and all the ingredients in a bowl.
2. Make 8 fudge balls out of this mixture.
3. Place the fudge balls in a baking sheet and refrigerate for 4 hours.
4. Serve.

Serving Suggestion: Serve the balls with chopped nuts on top.

Variation Tip: Add vanilla extracts to the dessert.

Nutritional Information Per Serving:

Calories 153 | Fat 1g |Sodium 8mg | Carbs 66g | Fiber 0.8g | Sugar 56g | Protein 1g

Brownie in a Tray

Prep Time: 15 minutes.
Cook Time: 1 minutes.
Serves: 4

Ingredients:

- 1 Medifast Brownie Mix
- 3 tablespoons water
- 1 wedge cream cheese
- 2 tablespoons Peanut butter powder
- 1 tablespoon water

Preparation:

6. Blend brownie mix with 3 tbs water in a shallow bowl.
7. Heat this mixture in the microwave for 1 minutes.
8. Slice the cream cheese slices and place on top of the brownie.
9. Blend peanut butter powder with 1 tablespoon water in a bowl.
10. Pour this mixture over the brownie.
11. Serve.

Serving Suggestion: Serve the brownie with chocolate syrup or berries on top.

Variation Tip: Add crushed walnuts or pecans to the brownie.

Nutritional Information Per Serving:

Calories 198 | Fat 14g |Sodium 272mg | Carbs 34g | Fiber 1g | Sugar 9.3g | Protein 1.3g

Dark Chocolate Mousse

Prep Time: 10 minutes.
Cook Time: 0 minutes.
Serves: 2

Ingredients:

- 2 ripe avocados, peeled and pitted
- ½ cup dark cocoa powder
- 1 tablespoon vanilla extract
- ¼ cup stevia powder
- ¼ cup almond milk
- 1 pinch salt

Preparation:

1. Blend all avocados with rest of the ingredients in a blender until smooth.
2. Cover and refrigerate the mousse for 1 hour.
3. Garnish and serve.

Serving Suggestion: Serve the mousse with chocolate sauce on top.

Variation Tip: Add crushed nuts or coconut flakes.

Nutritional Information Per Serving:

Calories 159 | Fat 3g |Sodium 277mg | Carbs 21g | Fiber 1g | Sugar 9g | Protein 2g

Banana Pudding

Prep Time: 10 minutes.
Cook Time: 15 minutes.
Serves: 4
Ingredients:
Cookie layer:

- 2 tablespoons butter softened
- 1 teaspoon vanilla extract
- 1 egg
- 1/2 cup almond flour
- 1 teaspoon baking powder
- 1/4 cup erythritol

Pudding layer:

- 2 cups heavy whipping cream
- 1 cup almond milk
- 2 teaspoons vanilla extract
- 6 egg yolks
- 1/2 cup erythritol
- 1 medium banana, sliced

Whipped cream layer:

- 1/2 cup heavy whipping cream
- 1 teaspoon vanilla extract
- 1/4 cup erythritol
- 1/4 teaspoon xanthan gum

Preparation:

1. At 350 degrees F, preheat your oven.
2. Layer a baking sheet with parchment paper.
3. Mix butter with egg and vanilla in a bowl.
4. Stir in baking powder, almond flour and erythritol then mix well.
5. Spread this mixture in an 8x16 inches baking sheet.
6. Bake this batter for 15 minutes until golden brown.
7. Meanwhile, mix all the pudding ingredients in a saucepan and cook until the pudding thickens.
8. Spread the pudding over the baked cookie layer.
9. Beat all the cream layer ingredients in a bowl until fluffy.
10. Spread this mixture over the pudding layer.
11. Cover and refrigerate for 1 hour.
12. Slice and serve.

Serving Suggestion: Serve the pudding cups with peanut butter frosting on top.

Variation Tip: Add chocolate chips or a teaspoon of crushed nuts to the batter for the change of flavor.

Nutritional Information Per Serving:
Calories 268 | Fat 14g |Sodium 122mg | Carbs 23.3g | Fiber 1.2g | Sugar 12g | Protein 6g

Lean and Green Recipes

Garlic Chicken with Zoodles

Prep Time: 15 minutes.
Cook Time: 28 minutes.
Serves: 4

Ingredients:

- 1 ½ lbs boneless chicken breasts
- 1 tablespoon olive oil
- 1 cup Greek yogurt
- ½ cup chicken broth
- ½ teaspoons garlic powder
- ½ teaspoons Italian seasoning
- ¼ cup parmesan cheese
- 1 cup spinach, chopped
- 6 sun-dried tomatoes slices
- 1 tablespoon garlic, chopped
- 1 ½ cups zucchini, cut into thin noodles

Preparation:

1. Pat dry the chicken breasts and rub them with cooking oil, black pepper and salt.
2. Sear the chicken in a skillet for 5 minutes per side until golden brown.
3. Transfer this prepared chicken to a plate and keep it aside.
4. Mix parmesan cheese, Italian seasoning, garlic powder, chicken broth and yogurt in a large skillet.
5. Mix and cook this mixture until it thickens.
6. Stir in sun-dried tomatoes and spinach, then cook for 3 minutes.
7. Toss in zucchini noodles and place the chicken on top.
8. At 350 degrees F, preheat your oven.
9. Bake the chicken and zucchini noodles for 15 minutes.
10. Serve warm.

Serving Suggestion: Serve the zoodles with a kale salad on the side.

Variation Tip: Coat the chicken with coconut shreds.

Nutritional Information Per Serving:
Calories 414 | Fat 15g |Sodium 587mg | Carbs 8g | Fiber 1g | Sugar 5g | Protein 60g

Chicken Zucchini Boats

Prep Time: 15 minutes.
Cook Time: 50 minutes.
Serves: 4

Ingredients:

- 4 zucchinis
- 1 lb. ground chicken
- 1/4 teaspoon salt
- 1/4 teaspoon black pepper
- 2 garlic cloves, minced

- 1 cup pasta sauce
- 1/4 cup parmesan cheese, grated
- 1/2 cup mozzarella cheese, shredded
- Sliced fresh basil for topping

Preparation:

1. At 400 degrees F, preheat your oven.
2. Layer a 9x13 inch baking pan with cooking spray.
3. Sauté chicken with black pepper and salt in a skillet for 10 minutes.
4. Add garlic and cook for 1 minute.
5. Stir in pasta sauce and sauté for 3 minutes.
6. Slice each zucchini boat in half, lengthwise and scoop out some flesh from the centre.
7. Divide the chicken into each zucchini half.
8. Place the prepared zucchini boats in the baking dish with cut-side up.
9. Sprinkle parmesan and mozzarella cheese on top.
10. Cover this baking dish with foil and bake for 35 minutes.
11. Sprinkle basil and serve.

Serving Suggestion: Serve the zucchini boats with fresh herbs on top and a bowl of steamed rice.

Variation Tip: Add some chopped bell pepper to the filling.

Nutritional Information Per Serving:
Calories 332 | Fat 18g |Sodium 611mg | Carbs 13.3g | Fiber 0g | Sugar g4 | Protein 38g

Medifast Chicken Fry

Prep Time: 15 minutes.
Cook Time: 10 minutes.
Serves: 4

Ingredients:

- 12 ounces boneless chicken breast
- 1 cup red bell pepper, chopped
- 1 cup green bell pepper, chopped
- 8 ounces broccoli slaw
- 1/2 cup chicken broth
- 2 tablespoons soy sauce
- 1 teaspoon crushed red pepper

Preparation:

1. Sauté broccoli slaw and peppers in a pan with chicken broth.
2. Stir in chicken, red pepper and soy sauce.
3. Cook for 10 minutes with occasional stirring.
4. Serve warm.

Serving Suggestion: Serve the stir fry with roasted green beans.

Variation Tip: Add some sliced onion and spring onion to the fry.

Nutritional Information Per Serving:
Calories 235 | Fat 5g |Sodium 422mg | Carbs 16g | Fiber 0g | Sugar 1g | Protein 25g

Tuscan Chicken

Prep Time: 15 minutes.
Cook Time: 23 minutes.
Serves: 4

Ingredients:

- 1 lb. boneless chicken breasts, sliced
- 2 tablespoons butter spread
- 4 cups kale leaves, chopped
- 2 garlic cloves, chopped
- 1 package Knorr rice sides cheddar broccoli
- ¼ cup sun-dried tomatoes, sliced
- Lemon wedges

Preparation:

1. Rub the chicken with black pepper and salt.
2. Sear the chicken with 1 tablespoon butter in a skillet for 5 minutes per side.
3. Transfer this prepared chicken to a plate and keep it aside.
4. Sauté garlic and kale with remaining butter in the same skillet over medium-high heat for 3 minutes.
5. Stir in 2 cup water and cheddar broccoli, and tomatoes then cook for 5 minutes with occasional stirring.
6. Return the cooked chicken to the skillet and cook for 5 minutes.
7. Garnish with lemon wedges and pine nuts.
8. Enjoy.

Serving Suggestion: Serve the chicken with roasted veggies.

Variation Tip: Replace kale with baby spinach if needed.

Nutritional Information Per Serving:

Calories 369 | Fat 14g |Sodium 442mg | Carbs 13.3g | Fiber 0.4g | Sugar 2g | Protein 32.3g

Chicken Taco Soup

Prep Time: 15 minutes.
Cook Time: 5 hours.
Serves: 4

Ingredients:

- 2 cups chicken broth
- 1/2 teaspoon cumin
- 2 cups of water
- 1 cup Rotel diced tomatoes
- 1 teaspoon taco seasoning
- 1/4 teaspoon chili powder
- 1 garlic clove, minced
- 14 ounces of raw chicken breasts
- 2 cups cabbage, chopped

Preparation:

1. Add all the taco soup ingredients to a crockpot.
2. Cover its lid and cook for 5 hours on low heat.
3. Shred the cooked chicken and return to the soup.
4. Serve warm.

Serving Suggestion: Serve the soup with fresh cucumber and couscous salad.

Variation Tip: Add some canned corn kernels to the soup.

Nutritional Information Per Serving:
Calories 453 | Fat 2.4g |Sodium 216mg | Carbs 18g | Fiber 2.3g | Sugar 1.2g | Protein 23.2g

Chicken Chili

Prep Time: 15 minutes.
Cook Time: 35 minutes.
Serves: 8

Ingredients:

- 8 (6 inches) corn tortillas
- 2 teaspoons vegetable oil
- 1 lb boneless chicken breast, diced
- 1 teaspoon ground cumin
- 1 cup poblano pepper, chopped
- 1/2 cup onion, chopped
- 1 garlic clove, minced
- 2 (14 ounces) cans of reduced-fat chicken broth
- 2 (15 ounces) cans of pinto beans
- 1 cups salsa Verde
- 2 tablespoons cilantro, minced

Preparation:

1. At 400 degrees F, preheat your oven.
2. Cut 4 the tortilla into ½ inch strips and toss them with 1 teaspoon oil.
3. Spread the tortillas on a baking sheet and bake for 12 minutes.
4. Grate the remaining tortillas into pieces and keep them aside.
5. Sauté chicken pieces with 1 teaspoon oil and cumin in a skillet for 5 minutes.
6. Transfer this prepared chicken to a plate and keep it aside.
7. Sauté garlic, onion and poblano peppers in the same skillet for 3 minutes.
8. Add grated tortillas, salsa, beans, broth and chicken, then cook for 15 minutes on a simmer.
9. Garnish with cilantro and baked tortillas.
10.   Serve warm.

Serving Suggestion: Serve the chili with toasted bread slices.

Variation Tip: Add corn kernels to the chicken chili.

Nutritional Information Per Serving:
Calories 354 | Fat 25g |Sodium 412mg | Carbs 22.3g | Fiber 0.2g | Sugar 1g | Protein 28.3g

Lean Green Chicken Soup

Prep Time: 15 minutes.
Cook Time: 25 minutes.
Serves: 6
Ingredients:

- 2 quarts chicken broth
- 1 1/2 lbs. boneless chicken breast
- 2 celery stalks, chopped
- 2 cups green beans, chopped

- 1 1/2 cups peas
- 2 cups asparagus, chopped
- 1 cup green onions, diced
- 6 garlic cloves, minced
- 2 cups spinach leaves, chopped
- 1 bunch watercress, chopped
- 1/2 cup parsley leaves, chopped
- 1/3 cup basil leaves, chopped
- 1 teaspoon salt
- 1/2 teaspoon black pepper

Preparation:

1. Boil chicken broth in a cooking pot and add chicken breasts.
2. Cook the chicken on a simmer for 15 minutes.
3. Stir in black pepper, salt, garlic, onions, asparagus, peas, green beans and celery.
4. Cook this mixture on a simmer for 10 minutes then remove from the heat.
5. Shred the cooked chicken with a fork.
6. Add basil, parsley, watercress and spinach to the soup.
7. Serve warm.

Serving Suggestion: Serve the soup with white rice or sweet potato salad.

Variation Tip: Add some zucchini noodles to the soup.

Nutritional Information Per Serving:
Calories 105 | Fat 15g |Sodium 852mg | Carbs 7g | Fiber 2g | Sugar 2g | Protein 15g

Avocado Chicken Salad

Prep Time: 15 minutes.
Cook Time: 0 minutes.
Serves: 4

Ingredients:

- 10 ounces cooked chicken breasts, sliced
- 1/2 cup Greek yogurt
- 3 ounces avocado, chopped
- 1/2 teaspoon garlic powder
- 1/4 teaspoon salt
- 1/8 teaspoons black pepper
- 1 tablespoon 1 teaspoon lime juice
- 1/4 cup fresh cilantro, chopped

Preparation:

1. Toss chicken with yogurt, avocado and the rest of the ingredients in a salad bowl.
2. Cover and refrigerate for 30 minutes.
3. Serve.

Serving Suggestion: Serve the salad with avocado guacamole on top.

Variation Tip: Add boiled peas to the salad.

Nutritional Information Per Serving:
Calories 352 | Fat 14g |Sodium 220mg | Carbs 16g | Fiber 0.2g | Sugar 1g | Protein 26g

Chicken Pesto Pasta

Prep Time: 15 minutes.
Cook Time: 0 minutes.
Serves: 6
Ingredients:

Kale Pesto

- 3 cups raw kale
- 2 cup fresh basil
- 2 tablespoons olive oil
- 3 tablespoons lemon juice
- 3 garlic cloves
- ¼ teaspoon salt

Pasta Salad

- 2 cups cooked chicken breast, diced
- 6 ounces cooked rotini chickpea pasta
- 1 cup arugula
- 3oz fresh mozzarella, diced

Preparation:

1. Blend kale with all the pesto ingredients in a blender until smooth.
2. Cook chicken cubes with pasta, arugula, pesto and mozzarella in a salad bowl.
3. Serve.

Serving Suggestion: Serve the pasta with a spinach salad.

Variation Tip: Add canned corns to the pasta.

Nutritional Information Per Serving:
Calories 388 | Fat 8g |Sodium 339mg | Carbs 8g | Fiber 1g | Sugar 2g | Protein 13g

Sesame Chicken Fry

Prep Time: 15 minutes.
Cook Time: 16 minutes.
Serves: 4
Ingredients:

For the sauce:

- 1/3 cup soy sauce
- ⅓ cup of water
- 3 garlic cloves, minced
- 2 tablespoons coconut sugar
- 1 tablespoon sesame oil
- 1 tablespoon rice vinegar
- 1 tablespoon fresh ginger, grated
- 1 tablespoon sesame seeds
- ½ teaspoon red pepper flakes
- ½ tablespoon arrowroot starch

For the chicken:

- 1/2 tablespoon sesame oil
- 1 lb. lean ground chicken
- ½ teaspoon garlic powder

- Salt and black pepper, to taste

For the veggies:

- ½ tablespoon toasted sesame oil
- 2 large carrots, sliced
- 1 white onion, chopped
- 1 red bell pepper, chopped
- 12 ounces green beans, trimmed

For serving

- ½ cup roasted cashews, chopped
- Scallions
- Extra sesame seeds

Preparation:

1. Mix soy sauce, arrowroot starch, red pepper flakes, sesame seeds, ginger, rice vinegar, sesame oil, coconut sugar, garlic, and water in a bowl.
2. Sauté ground chicken with ½ tablespoons sesame oil in a large pot until golden brown.
3. Stir in black pepper, salt and garlic powder.
4. Transfer this meat to a bowl and keep it aside.
5. Sauté onion with carrots and ½ tablespoons sesame oil in the same pan for 4 minutes.
6. Stir in green beans and bell pepper then cook for 8 minutes.
7. Return the chicken to the veggies and cook for 4 minutes.
8. Serve with brown rice or quinoa.
9. Garnish with roasted cashews, scallions and sesame seeds.
10. Enjoy.

Serving Suggestion: Serve the chicken fry with steaming white rice.

Variation Tip: Add roasted peanuts on top.

Nutritional Information Per Serving:

Calories 301 | Fat 16g |Sodium 189mg | Carbs 32g | Fiber 0.3g | Sugar 0.1g | Protein 28.2g

Teriyaki Chicken Broccoli

Prep Time: 15 minutes.
Cook Time: 13 minutes.
Serves: 4

Ingredients:

- 10 ounces chicken strips
- 2 tablespoons teriyaki sauce
- 1 tablespoon fresh garlic, minced
- 1/2 cup yellow onion, diced
- 2 cups broccoli, florets
- 1/4 cup fresh scallions. sliced
- 2 tablespoons water

Preparation:

1. Sauté onion and garlic in a non-stick skillet for 5 minutes.
2. Stir in chicken and the rest of the ingredients, then cook for 8 minutes.
3. Serve warm.

Serving Suggestion: Serve the chicken broccoli with cauliflower rice.

Variation Tip: Add dried herbs to the mixture for seasoning.

Nutritional Information Per Serving:

Calories 231 | Fat 20g |Sodium 941mg | Carbs 30g | Fiber 0.9g | Sugar 1.4g | Protein 14.6g

White Chicken Chili

Prep Time: 15 minutes.
Cook Time: 8 hours.
Serves: 6

Ingredients:

- 3 boneless chicken breasts
- 2 (15 ½ ounce) cans great northern beans
- 1 (15 ounce) of sweet golden corn
- 1 (4 ½ ounce) can green chiles, chopped
- 2 (14.5 ounce) cans chicken broth
- 1 sweet yellow onion, chopped
- 3 garlic cloves, minced
- 1 lime, juiced
- 1 teaspoon cumin
- 1/2 teaspoon onion powder
- 1/2 teaspoon garlic powder
- 1 1/2 teaspoon chilli powder
- 1/4 teaspoon cayenne pepper
- Black pepper, to taste
- Paprika, to taste

Preparation:

1. Add chicken, beans and all other ingredients to a crockpot.
2. Cover and cook the chicken chilli for 8 hours on Low.
3. Shred this cooked chicken with two forks and return to the chili.
4. Garnish with your favorite toppings.
5. Enjoy.

Serving Suggestion: Serve the chicken chilli with a fresh crouton's salad.

Variation Tip: Add a drizzle of cheese on top.

Nutritional Information Per Serving:

Calories 300 | Fat 2g |Sodium 374mg | Carbs 30g | Fiber 6g | Sugar 3g | Protein 32g

Chicken Thighs with Green Olive

Prep Time: 15 minutes.
Cook Time: 20 minutes.
Serves: 4

Ingredients:

- 1 ½ lb. boneless chicken thighs, trimmed
- ¼ teaspoon salt
- ¼ teaspoon black pepper
- ¼ cup all-purpose flour
- 3/4 cup cranberry juice
- 1 tablespoon 1 teaspoon olive oil
- 4 garlic cloves, minced
- ¾ cup chicken broth

- 1/4 cup dried cherries
- ¼ cup sliced green olives. pitted
- 2 tablespoons red-wine vinegar
- 1 tablespoon brown sugar
- 1 teaspoon dried oregano

Preparation:

1. Rub the chicken with black pepper and salt, then coat with the flour.
2. Mix ¼ cup cranberry juice with 4 teaspoons flour in a bowl until smooth.
3. Sear the seasoned chicken in 1 tablespoon oil in a skillet over medium heat for 5 minutes per side.
4. Transfer the prepared chicken to a plate and keep them aside.
5. Stir in garlic, 1 teaspoon oil, and sauté for 30 seconds.
6. Add flour juice mixture, ½ cup cranberry juice, cherries, oregano, brown sugar, vinegar and olives.
7. Boil this mixture, reduce the heat, simmer and cook for 6 minutes with occasional stirring.
8. Return this chicken to the pan and cook for 2 minutes.
9. Serve warm.

Serving Suggestion: Serve the chicken with toasted bread slices.

Variation Tip: Add butter sauce on top of the chicken before cooking.

Nutritional Information Per Serving:
Calories 419 | Fat 13g |Sodium 432mg | Carbs 9.1g | Fiber 3g | Sugar 1g | Protein 33g

Chicken Divan

Prep Time: 15 minutes.
Cook Time: 41 minutes.
Serves: 8

Ingredients:

- 2 tablespoons olive oil
- 1 lb. boneless chicken breast, diced
- 1 large onion, diced
- 3 garlic cloves, minced
- ¾ teaspoon salt
- ½ teaspoon black pepper
- ½ teaspoon dry thyme
- ¼ cup dry sherry
- 2 cups chicken broth
- ¼ cup all-purpose flour
- 2/3 cup Parmesan cheese, grated
- ¼ cup sour cream
- 2 pieces Broccoli crowns, chopped
- ½ cup water
- 3 tablespoons panko
- ½ teaspoon paprika

Preparation:

1. At 400 degrees F, preheat your oven.

2. Grease a 2 ½ quart baking dish with cooking spray.
3. Sauté chicken with 1 tablespoon oil in a skillet until golden brown for 10 minutes.
4. Transfer to a plate, cover with a foil and keep aside.
5. Sauté onion, thyme, black pepper, salt and garlic with 2 teaspoons oil in the same skillet for 4 minutes.
6. Stir in sherry then cook a simmer for 3 minutes.
7. Pour in 1 ½ cup broth then cook on a simmer with occasional stirring.
8. Mix flour with ½ cup broth in a bowl and pour into the skillet.
9. Cook until the mixture thickens then add sour cream and 1/3 cup parmesan.
10. Return the chicken to the mixture and mix well
11. Add broccoli and ½ cup water to a bowl, cover and microwave for 2 minutes.
12. Drain and transfer the broccoli to the chicken then mix well.
13. Spread this chicken mixture in the prepared casserole dish.
14. Drizzle remaining parmesan, panko, paprika and 1 teaspoon oil on top.
15. Bake for 22 minutes in the preheated oven.
16. Serve warm.

Serving Suggestion: Serve the chicken divan with roasted veggies on the side.

Variation Tip: Add peas and corn to the casserole.

Nutritional Information Per Serving:
Calories 334 | Fat 16g |Sodium 462mg | Carbs 31g | Fiber 0.4g | Sugar 3g | Protein 35.3g

Spicy Taco Meat

Prep Time: 15 minutes.
Cook Time: 16 minutes.
Serves: 6
Ingredients:

- 8 ounces lean ground beef
- 8 ounces lean ground turkey breast
- ½ cup onion, chopped
- 1 (10-ounce) can dice tomatoes
- ½ teaspoon ground cumin
- 1/2 teaspoon ground chipotle chile
- ½ teaspoon dried oregano

Preparation:

1. Sauté onion, turkey and beef in a skillet over medium heat for 10 minutes.
2. Transfer the mixture to a plate and keep it aside.
3. Stir in tomatoes, oregano, cumin and chipotle.
4. Sauté for 6 minutes then return the meat mixture.
5. Serve warm.

Serving Suggestion: Serve the taco meat with mashed sweet potato and roasted asparagus on the side.

Variation Tip: Use chicken mince instead of beef.

Nutritional Information Per Serving:
Calories 305 | Fat 25g |Sodium 532mg | Carbs 2.3g | Fiber 0.4g | Sugar 2g | Protein 18.3g

Taco Salad

Prep Time: 15 minutes.
Cook Time: 10 minutes.
Serves: 6

Ingredients:

- 1 lb. lean ground beef
- 1 tablespoon chili powder
- 8 green onions, chopped,
- 1 head romaine lettuce, chopped
- 1 medium tomato, chopped
- 1 avocado, diced
- 1 4-ounce can olives, sliced
- 1 1/2 cups cheddar cheese, grated
- 1/2 cup plain yogurt
- 1/2 cup salsa

Preparation:

1. Sauté beef with black pepper, salt, onions, and chili powder in a skillet until brown.
2. Transfer to a salad bowl then toss in remaining ingredients.
3. Serve.

Serving Suggestion: Serve the salad with toasted bread slices.

Variation Tip: Add crumbled feta cheese on top.

Nutritional Information Per Serving:

Calories 325 | Fat 16g | Sodium 431mg | Carbs 22g | Fiber 1.2g | Sugar 4g | Protein 23g

Beef Broccoli

Prep Time: 15 minutes.
Cook Time: 44 minutes.
Serves: 2

Ingredients:

- 1 cup brown rice
- 1 1/2 cups water
- 1/4 cup soy sauce
- 2 tablespoons brown sugar
- 1 tablespoon fresh ginger, grated
- 2 teaspoons rice wine vinegar
- 1 teaspoon sesame oil
- 1 teaspoon sriracha sauce
- 1 tablespoon canola oil
- 1 lb. boneless beef, diced
- 3 garlic cloves, minced
- 2 cups broccoli florets
- 1/4 cup green onions, sliced
- Sesame seeds to garnish

Preparation:

1. Boil rice with water in a pan then cook on low heat for 30 minutes.
2. Mix sriracha, sesame oil. Rice wine vinegar, ginger, brown sugar, and soy sauce in a small bowl.
3. Sauté beef with garlic and oil in a skillet for 10 minutes.

4. Transfer to a plate and keep it aside.
5. Add soy sauce mixture, cooked rice, green onions and broccoli to the same skillet.
6. Cook for 4 minutes then divide in the serving plates.
7. Add meat mixture on top and garnish with sesame seeds.
8. Serve warm.

Serving Suggestion: Serve this beef broccoli with cauliflower rice.

Variation Tip: Add toasted croutons on top.

Nutritional Information Per Serving:
Calories 425 | Fat 14g |Sodium 411mg | Carbs 44g | Fiber 0.3g | Sugar 1g | Protein 28.3g

Beef Bake

Prep Time: 15 minutes.
Cook Time: 35 minutes.
Serves: 6
Ingredients:

- 12 ounces cauliflower rice
- 1 ½ lb lean ground beef
- 15 ounces can of tomato sauce
- ½ cup sour cream
- 1 ¼ cup cottage cheese, shredded
- 2 cups cheddar cheese, shredded
- 1/2 cup green onions, sliced
- 1 teaspoon salt
- 1 teaspoon black pepper

Preparation:

1. At 350 degrees F, preheat your oven.
2. Spread cauliflower rice in a 2 ½ quart baking dish then heat for 5 minutes in the microwave.
3. Sauté beef with oil in a skillet for 10 minutes until brown.
4. Stir in tomato sauce, black pepper and salt.
5. Mix cottage cheese, sour cream, and green onions in a bowl.
6. Spread half of the beef mixture on top cauliflower rice.
7. Top it with half of the cheese mixture then add another layer of beef.
8. Finally add the remaining cheese mixture on top.
9. Bake this casserole for 20 minutes at 350 degrees F, in the preheated oven.
10.   Serve warm.

Serving Suggestion: Serve the beef bake with sweet potato salad.

Variation Tip: Add breadcrumbs to the topping for more crispiness.

Nutritional Information Per Serving:
Calories 425 | Fat 15g |Sodium 345mg | Carbs 12.3g | Fiber 1.4g | Sugar 3g | Protein 23.3g

Ground Beef Salad

Prep Time: 15 minutes.
Cook Time: 39 minutes.
Serves: 4
Ingredients:

Taco Ground Beef

- 1 tablespoon olive oil
- 1 ½ lbs lean ground beef

- 1 cup white onion, diced
- ½ cup red bell pepper
- 3 garlic cloves, minced
- 1 teaspoon paprika
- 1 tablespoon onion powder
- 1 teaspoon coriander powder
- 1 teaspoon chili powder
- 1 teaspoon cumin powder
- 1 tablespoon dried oregano
- 1/2 teaspoon cayenne pepper
- Salt and black pepper to taste
- 1 cup chicken broth

Salsa

- 2 medium tomatoes, diced
- ¼ cup red onion, diced
- 1 green bell pepper, diced
- 1 teaspoon jalapeno, chopped
- Fresh cilantro, chopped
- 1 tablespoon lime juice
- 1 small garlic clove, minced
- Salt and pepper to taste

Salad

- 6 cups romaine lettuce, chopped
- ½ avocado, sliced
- lime wedges, for garnish
- Salt and black pepper to taste
- Cilantro for garnish

Preparation:

1. Sauté beef with olive oil in a large pot until brown.
2. Stir in bell pepper and onion then sauté for 8 minutes.
3. Toss in garlic then cook for almost 30 seconds then add all the spices.
4. Mix well then stir in chicken stock ten cook to a boil.
5. Reduce its heat, cover and cook for 30 minutes with occasional stirring.
6. Mix all the salsa ingredients in a bowl, cover and refrigerate for 30 minutes.
7. Toss all lettuces and salad ingredients in a salad bowl.
8. Stir in cooked beef then mix well.
9. Add salsa on top and garnish with cilantro.
10. Enjoy.

Serving Suggestion: Serve the beef salad with roasted asparagus.

Variation Tip: Add a drizzle of parmesan cheese on top.

Nutritional Information Per Serving:
Calories 91 | Fat 5g |Sodium 88mg | Carbs 3g | Fiber 0g | Sugar 0g | Protein 7g

Veggie Beef Stir-Fry

Prep Time: 15 minutes.
Cook Time: 20 minutes.
Serves: 4

Ingredients:

- 12 ounces frozen riced cauliflower
- 1 lb. lean Ground Beef
- 2 tablespoons canola oil
- 1 cup baby Bella mushrooms
- 1 cup green beans, trimmed
- 1 cup matchstick carrots
- 2 garlic cloves, minced
- ¼ cup soy sauce
- ¼ cup teriyaki sauce
- 1 tablespoon brown sugar

Preparation:

1. Add cauliflower rice to a bowl and heat in the microwave for 2 minutes then drain.
2. Sauté beef with cooking oil in a skillet for 10 minutes then remove from the heat.
3. Add mushrooms, garlic, carrots, and green beans then sauté for 5 minutes.
4. Stir in brown sugar, teriyaki sauce and soy sauce then cook for 3 minutes.
5. Serve warm with cauliflower rice.

Serving Suggestion: Serve the stir fry with cauliflower rice.

Variation Tip: Add a layer of the boiled zucchini noodles to the stir fry.

Nutritional Information Per Serving:
Calories 276 | Fat 21g |Sodium 476mg | Carbs 12g | Fiber 3g | Sugar 4g | Protein 10g

Ground Beef Over Zoodles

Prep Time: 15 minutes.
Cook Time: 11 minutes.
Serves: 4

Ingredients:

Meat

- 1 lb lean ground beef
- 1 small onion, chopped
- 1 garlic clove, chopped
- 1 jalapeno pepper, chopped
- 1/2 teaspoon salt
- 1/2 teaspoon black pepper
- 1/2 teaspoon onion powder
- 1/2 teaspoon smoked paprika
- 1/2 teaspoon ground coriander
- 1 teaspoon dried oregano
- 1/2 cup bone broth
- 1 medium tomato, chopped

Zoodles

- 2 zucchinis, spiralized
- 1/4 teaspoon salt
- 1/4 teaspoon black pepper

- 1/4 teaspoon garlic powder
- 1/2 teaspoon dried oregano

Preparation:

1. Sauté ground beef with black pepper, and salt in a cooking pot for 8 minutes until brown.
2. Stir in jalapeno pepper, garlic and onion then sauté for 1 minute.
3. Add spices and water then cook for 1 minute then add tomato.
4. Transfer the mixture to a plate then add zucchini noodles.
5. Stir in garlic powder, black pepper and salt then sauté for 30 seconds.
6. Serve warm.

Serving Suggestion: Serve the beef zoodles with a fresh green's salad.

Variation Tip: Add chopped herbs on top.

Nutritional Information Per Serving:
Calories 487 | Fat 24g |Sodium 686mg | Carbs 17g | Fiber 1g | Sugar 1.2g | Protein 52g

Mediterranean Beef and Rice

Prep Time: 15 minutes.
Cook Time: 14 minutes.
Serves: 4

Ingredients:

- 10 ounces lean ground beef
- 1/2 cup rice, rinsed and drained
- 1 onion, chopped
- 1 garlic clove, minced
- 1 tablespoon olive oil
- 1 small tomato, chopped
- 1 teaspoon cumin
- 1 teaspoon coriander
- 1 teaspoon mint
- 1 teaspoon paprika
- 1 cup green beans

Preparation:

1. Sauté beef with oil in a skillet for 3 minutes then add paprika, mint, coriander and cumin.
2. Mix well and toss in garlic and onion.
3. Sauté for 1 minute then add 1/3 cup water, a pinch of salt and rice.
4. Cover this pan and cook for 10 minutes on a simmer.
5. Stir in tomato and green beans then cook until the rice is done.
6. Garnish as desired and serve warm.

Serving Suggestion: Serve the beef rice with sweet potato salad.

Variation Tip: Drizzle parmesan cheese on top before serving.

Nutritional Information Per Serving:
Calories 255 | Fat 12g |Sodium 66mg | Carbs 13g | Fiber 2g | Sugar 4g | Protein 22g

Beef Stew with Green Beans

Prep Time: 15 minutes.
Cook Time: 2 hours.
Serves: 8

Ingredients:

- 6 tablespoons olive oil
- 4 ½ lbs. lean beef stew, cut into cubes
- 3 ½ lbs. green beans
- 1 large onion, minced
- 3 garlic cloves, minced
- 1 large ripe tomato, grated
- 3 tablespoons tomato paste
- 2 tablespoons olive oil
- 1 handful of parsley, chopped
- 2 dried bay leaves
- Salt and black pepper, to taste

Preparation:

1. Sauté meat with olive oil in a cooking pot over high heat until brown.
2. Transfer the meat to a plate and keep it aside.
3. Add garlic and onion to the same pot and sauté until soft.
4. Stir in grated tomato, tomato paste and 1 cup water.
5. Mix this well then return the meat to the pot and cover with enough water.
6. Cook this mixture for 1 hour until meat is tender.
7. Stir in bay leaves, black pepper, salt, parsley and green beans.
8. Cook for 1 hour more hour and serve warm.

Serving Suggestion: Serve the beef stew with fresh herbs on top.

Variation Tip: Add butter to the meat before serving.

Nutritional Information Per Serving:
Calories 405 | Fat 22.7g |Sodium 227mg | Carbs 26.1g | Fiber 1.4g | Sugar 0.9g | Protein 45.2g

Ground Beef Skillet

Prep Time: 15 minutes.
Cook Time: 70 minutes.
Serves: 4

Ingredients:

- 1 spaghetti squash
- 2 teaspoons olive oil
- Salt, black pepper, and garlic powder to taste
- 1 lb. lean ground beef
- 1 small onion, diced
- 1 bell pepper, diced
- 3 garlic cloves, minced
- 1 cup baby Bella mushrooms, chopped
- 2 (15 ounces) canned diced tomatoes
- 1 (15 ounces) can of tomato sauce
- 1 tablespoon Italian seasoning
- Salt and black pepper to taste
- 1/4 cup basil, chopped

- 2 tablespoons parmesan cheese

Preparation:

1. At 400 degrees F, preheat your oven.
2. Cut the prepared squash in half; lengthwise, remove the seed and rub it with garlic powder, black pepper, salt and olive oil.
3. Place the cut squash with the skin side down in a baking sheet and roast for 40 minutes in the preheated oven.
4. Scrap out the roasted squash with a fork and transfer to a plate.
5. Sauté beef in a skillet until brown.
6. Stir in pepper and onion, then sauté for 5 minutes.
7. Add garlic, mushrooms, black pepper and salt, then sauté for 5 minutes.
8. Stir in Italian seasoning, tomato sauce and diced tomatoes.
9. Cook for 20 minutes, then garnish with parsley.
10. Serve the beef on top of the spaghetti squash.
11. Enjoy.

Serving Suggestion: Serve the beef with sautéed carrots on the side.

Variation Tip: Drizzle parmesan cheese on top before serving.

Nutritional Information Per Serving:
Calories 345 | Fat 36g |Sodium 272mg | Carbs 41g | Fiber 0.2g | Sugar 0.1g | Protein 22.5g

Steak with Onions

Prep Time: 15 minutes.
Cook Time: 12 minutes.
Serves: 2

Ingredients:

- 5 ounces lean beef steak
- 1 small onion
- 1 small tomato, halved
- 1 cup spinach
- 1 teaspoon rosemary
- 1 teaspoon olive oil
- Salt and black pepper to taste

Preparation:

1. Sauté onion with oil in a large skillet until soft.
2. Stir in rosemary, and sauté until brown.
3. Add tomato to the skillet and steak to the skillet.
4. Cook for 9 minutes and flip the steaks once cooked halfway through.
5. Add spinach to the steaks and cook for 3 minutes.
6. Serve warm.

Serving Suggestion: Serve the steaks with sautéed green beans and mashed sweet potatoes.

Variation Tip: Drizzle parmesan cheese on top before cooking.

Nutritional Information Per Serving:
Calories 395 | Fat 9.5g |Sodium 655mg | Carbs 13.4g | Fiber 0.4g | Sugar 0.4g | Protein 28.3g

Meatloaf

Prep Time: 15 minutes.
Cook Time: 9 minutes.
Serves: 6

Ingredients:

- 1 onion
- 1 ½ lbs of extra lean ground beef
- 1 cup zucchini, shredded
- ¾ cup green pepper diced
- 1 egg
- 5 teaspoons Worcestershire sauce
- 3 teaspoons grainy mustard
- 2 tablespoons ketchup
- ½ cup breadcrumb
- 1 teaspoon smoked paprika
- ½ teaspoons salt
- ½ teaspoons black pepper

Preparation:

1. At 375 degrees F, preheat your oven.
2. Beat egg with black pepper, paprika, salt, Worcestershire sauce, and mustard in a large bowl.
3. Stir in breadcrumbs and vegetables.
4. Add beef, mix well and spread this meat mixture into a loaf pan.
5. Cover the meat mixture with ketchup on top.
6. Bake the meatloaf for 9 minutes in the oven.
7. Slice and serve warm.

Serving Suggestion: Serve the meatloaf with fresh green and mashed sweet potatoes.

Variation Tip: Skip zucchini and replace it with an equal amount of shredded carrot.

Nutritional Information Per Serving:
Calories 301 | Fat 5g |Sodium 340mg | Carbs 24.7g | Fiber 1.2g | Sugar 1.3g | Protein 15.3g

BBQ Beef with Sweet Potato Salad

Prep Time: 15 minutes.
Cook Time: 10 hours 8 minutes.
Serves: 4

Ingredients:

For the BBQ Beef:

- 2 lbs. top round beef, diced
- 1 large onion, chopped
- 28 ounces canned tomato puree
- 1 tablespoon chilli powder
- 1 tablespoon dried thyme
- 1/2 teaspoon garlic powder
- 1/2 teaspoon black pepper

Sweet Potato Salad

- 1 1/2 lb. sweet potatoes, diced
- 2 stalk celery, chopped
- 2 green onions, chopped

- 2 tablespoon light mayonnaise
- 1/3 cup fat-free, plain yogurt
- 2 teaspoon apple cider vinegar
- 1/8 teaspoon black pepper

Preparation:

1. Mix all the BBQ beef ingredients in a large bowl.
2. Transfer this mixture to a slow cooker, cover and cook for 10 hours on low heat setting.
3. Meanwhile, cook chopped sweet potatoes with water for 8 minutes until soft.
4. Drain and toss the boiled sweet potatoes with the remaining salad ingredients in a bowl.
5. Serve the BBQ beef with the sweet potatoes.
6. Enjoy.

Serving Suggestion: Serve the beef with roasted green beans.

Variation Tip: Add barbecue sauce to the beef.

Nutritional Information Per Serving:

Calories 448 | Fat 23g |Sodium 350mg | Carbs 18g | Fiber 6.3g | Sugar 1g | Protein 40.3g

Green Beans with Pork and Potatoes

Prep Time: 15 minutes.
Cook Time: 22 minutes.
Serves: 4

Ingredients:

- 1 lb. lean pork, cubed
- 1 large onion, chopped
- 1/2 cup olive oil
- 2 carrots, sliced
- 2 celery sticks, sliced
- 3 fresh tomatoes, grated
- 1 lb. green beans
- 2 potatoes, peeled and cut into quarters
- 1/2 teaspoon salt
- 1/2 teaspoon black pepper

Preparation:

1. Sauté pork with oil in an Instant Pot for 5 minutes on a Sauté mode.
2. Stir in all the veggies and the rest of the ingredients.
3. Cover the lid and cook on a Manual Setting for 17 minutes.
4. Once done, release the pressure completely, then remove the lid.
5. Serve warm.

Serving Suggestion: Serve the pork with toasted bread slices.

Variation Tip: Replace potatoes with sweet potatoes.

Nutritional Information Per Serving:

Calories 309 | Fat 25g |Sodium 463mg | Carbs 9.9g | Fiber 0.3g | Sugar 0.3g | Protein 18g

Roasted Pork Chops

Prep Time: 15 minutes.
Cook Time: 16 minutes.
Serves: 6
Ingredients:

- 1 ½ teaspoons paprika
- 1 ½ teaspoons dried ginger
- 1 ½ teaspoons dried mustard
- 1 ½ teaspoons kosher salt
- 1 ½ teaspoons ground black pepper
- 1 ½ tablespoons olive oil
- 6 thick-cut bone-in pork chops

Ginger Green Beans

- 1 ½ tablespoons olive oil
- 2 lb. green beans, de-stemmed
- 1/4 teaspoon crushed red pepper flakes
- 1 teaspoon dried ginger
- 3 teaspoons soy sauce

Preparation:

1. At 500 degrees F, preheat your oven.
2. Mix paprika, black pepper, brown sugar, kosher salt, dried mustard and 1 teaspoon dried ginger in a bowl.
3. Rub the pork chops with the spice rub mixture.
4. Preheat a skillet with 1 tablespoon oil over high heat.
5. Sear the pork chops for almost 2 minutes per side.
6. Roast these chops 6 minutes in the oven, and flip once cooked halfway through.
7. Meanwhile, sauté green beans with 1 tablespoon olive oil in a skillet for 1 minute.
8. Stir in red pepper flakes, soy sauce, ½ teaspoons dried ginger and cook for 5 minutes.
9. Serve the cooked pork chops with the green beans.
10. Enjoy.

Serving Suggestion: Serve the pork chops with roasted green beans.

Variation Tip: Add paprika for more spice.

Nutritional Information Per Serving:

Calories 537 | Fat 20g |Sodium 719mg | Carbs 25.1g | Fiber 0.9g | Sugar 1.4g | Protein 37.8g

Roasted Shrimp and Green Beans

Prep Time: 15 minutes.
Cook Time: 20 minutes.
Serves: 4
Ingredients:

For the beans:

- 1 lb. green beans, chopped
- 1 tablespoon olive oil
- ½ teaspoons ground coriander
- ½ teaspoons ground cumin
- ¼ teaspoons kosher salt
- ½ teaspoons black pepper
- 1/8 teaspoons Cayenne pepper

For the shrimp:

- 1 lb. raw shrimp, peeled
- 1 tablespoon olive oil
- zest from one lemon
- 1/4 teaspoon salt
- 1/2 teaspoon black pepper

Preparation:

1. At 425 degrees F, preheat your oven.
2. Toss beans with cayenne pepper, black pepper, salt, cumin, coriander, and olive oil in a bowl.
3. Toss shrimp with black pepper, salt, lemon zest, and oil in another bowl.
4. Grease a baking sheet with oil and spread the green beans in this sheet.
5. Roast these beans for 10 minutes, toss and add shrimp on top.
6. Continue baking for 10 minutes.
7. Garnish with lemon quarters.
8. Serve warm.

Serving Suggestion: Serve the shrimp with cauliflower rice risotto.

Variation Tip: Add paprika for more spice.

Nutritional Information Per Serving:
Calories 212 | Fat 9g |Sodium 353mg | Carbs 8g | Fiber 3g | Sugar 4g | Protein 25g

Shrimp Scampi

Prep Time: 15 minutes.
Cook Time: 14 minutes.
Serves: 6
Ingredients:

- 2 tablespoons butter
- 1/2 cup onion, diced
- 3 garlic cloves, minced
- 1 teaspoon dried oregano
- 1 teaspoon dried basil
- 1 teaspoon cayenne pepper
- 1 lb. raw shrimp, peeled and deveined
- 3 tablespoons fresh parsley
- Squeeze of lemon

Preparation:

1. Sauté garlic, spices and onion with butter in a skillet for 7 minutes.
2. Stir in shrimp and sauté for 4 minutes.
3. Add lemon juice and parsley.
4. Serve warm.

Serving Suggestion: Serve the scampi with zucchini noodles.

Variation Tip: Add mixed chopped herbs and lemon zest to the scampi.

Nutritional Information Per Serving:
Calories 376 | Fat 17g |Sodium 1127mg | Carbs 24g | Fiber 1g | Sugar 3g | Protein 29g

Grilled Shrimp Kabobs

Prep Time: 15 minutes.
Cook Time: 10 minutes.
Serves: 4
Ingredients:

- ¼ cup lemon juice
- ¼ cup vegetable oil
- 1 tablespoon thyme, chopped
- ¼ teaspoon salt
- ¼ teaspoon pepper
- ¾ lb. sea scallops
- 12 large uncooked shrimp
- 8 medium whole fresh mushrooms
- 8 cherry tomatoes
- 1 medium zucchini, cut into slices

Preparation:

1. Set a grill over medium heat.
2. Mix lemon juice with black pepper, salt, oil and thyme in a bowl.
3. Cut all the scallops in half.
4. Thread scallops, zucchini, tomatoes, shrimp and mushrooms on the skewers alternately.
5. Brush the skewers with a lemon juice mixture.
6. Grill these skewers for 10 minutes while basting with lemon mixture and turning the skewers around.
7. Serve warm.

Serving Suggestion: Serve the shrimp skewers with fresh greens on the side.

Variation Tip: Roll the shrimp and scallops in breadcrumbs for a crispy touch.

Nutritional Information Per Serving:
Calories 457 | Fat 19g |Sodium 557mg | Carbs 19g | Fiber 1.8g | Sugar 1.2g | Protein 32.5g

Goan Fish Curry

Prep Time: 15 minutes.
Cook Time: 11 minutes.
Serves: 2
Ingredients:

- 3 garlic cloves, chopped
- 3 cm ginger, chopped
- 1 green chilli, chopped
- 2 tomatoes, chopped
- 1 tablespoon coconut oil
- 1 red onion, diced
- 1 tablespoon garam masala
- 1 tablespoon ground cumin
- 1 x 400ml tin coconut milk
- 1 lb. haddock fillet, cut into chunks
- Juice of 1 lime
- ½ bunch of coriander, chopped

Preparation:

1. Blend tomatoes with chilli, ginger and garlic in a food processor until smooth.
2. Sauté onion with oil in a wok for 2 minutes.

3. Stir in cumin and garam masala then cook for 30 seconds.
4. Add the tomato mixture and coconut milk then boil the mixture.
5. Reduce the heat, and cook for 2 minutes on a simmer.
6. Place the haddock pieces in the curry, cook for 6 minutes on a simmer.
7. Garnish with coriander and lime juice.
8. Serve warm.

Serving Suggestion: Serve the curry with cauliflower rice.

Variation Tip: Replace haddock with codfish if needed.

Nutritional Information Per Serving:
Calories 392 | Fat 16g |Sodium 466mg | Carbs 3.9g | Fiber 0.9g | Sugar 0.6g | Protein 48g

Fish Pie

Prep Time: 15 minutes.
Cook Time: 37 minutes.
Serves: 4

Ingredients:

- 3/4-pint semi-skimmed milk
- 2 bay leaves
- 3 spring onions, chopped
- 3 tablespoons corn flour
- 1 teaspoon Dijon mustard
- 2 tablespoons dill, chopped
- 5 ½ ounces cod, cut into chunks
- 5 ½ ounces smoked haddock, cut into chunks
- 5 ½ ounces salmon, cut into chunks
- 5 ounces raw king prawns
- 3 ½ ounces frozen peas
- 2 potatoes, peeled
- 2 tablespoons olive oil
- 1-ounce vintage Cheddar, grated
- Steamed broccoli, to serve

Preparation:

1. At 350 degrees F, preheat your oven.
2. Boil milk with spring onion and bay leaves in a cooking pot.
3. Mix corn flour with 3 tablespoons cold water in a bowl.
4. Pour into the milk and cook for 4 minutes with occasional stirring until thickens.
5. Stir in dill, and mustard then cook for 2 minutes then discard the bay leaves.
6. Add prawns, peas and fish mix, spread this mixture in a casserole dish.
7. Boil potatoes in salted water for 1 minute then grate them.
8. Mix grated potatoes with olive oil, cheese and seasoning in a bowl.
9. Spread these potatoes on top of the seafood mixture.
10.   Bake this pie for 30 minutes in the oven until golden brown.
11.   Serve warm.

Serving Suggestion: Serve the fish pie with cauliflower salad.

Variation Tip: Add some cream cheese to the pie filling.

Nutritional Information Per Serving:
Calories 321 | Fat 7.4g |Sodium 356mg | Carbs 9.3g | Fiber 2.4g | Sugar 5g | Protein 37.2g

Parmesan Shrimp Zoodles

Prep Time: 15 minutes.
Cook Time: 18 minutes.
Serves: 4
Ingredients:

- 16 ounces medium shrimp
- 1 cup cherry tomatoes, cut in half
- 8 cups zucchini noodles
- 3 tablespoons olive oil
- 2 tablespoons garlic, minced
- 1/2 cup Parmesan cheese, grated
- 1 teaspoon dried oregano
- 1/2 teaspoon chili powder
- 1/2 teaspoon salt
- 1/2 teaspoon black pepper

Preparation:

1. At 400 degrees F, preheat your oven.
2. Layer a baking sheet with foil sheet.
3. Rinse the shrimp in a colander and leave for 5 minutes.
4. Mix parmesan cheese with black pepper, salt, chili powder, and oregano in a bowl.
5. Drain the shrimp and toss with 1 tablespoon garlic and 1 tablespoon oil in a bowl.
6. Drizzle half of the cheese mixture on top of the shrimp.
7. Mix well and drizzle the remaining cheese on top.
8. Spread the shrimp on the baking sheet and bake for 10 minutes.
9. Sauté garlic with remaining oil, zucchini noodles and tomatoes in a skillet for 8 minutes.
10. Serve the shrimp with zucchini noodles and garnish with parmesan cheese.

Serving Suggestion: Serve the shrimp noodles with sautéed vegetables.

Variation Tip: Add canned corn to the shrimp.

Nutritional Information Per Serving:
Calories 258 | Fat 9g |Sodium 994mg | Carbs 1g | Fiber 0.4g | Sugar 3g | Protein 16g

Shrimp and Cauliflower Grits with Greens

Prep Time: 15 minutes.
Cook Time: 20 minutes.
Serves: 4
Ingredients:

Cauliflower Grits

- 1 head cauliflower
- 2 tablespoons avocado oil
- 1 cup of coconut milk
- 1/2 teaspoon sea salt
- 1 tablespoon tapioca starch
- 2 tablespoons water
- 1/2 cup white cheddar, grated

Sautéed Greens

- 1 tablespoon avocado oil

- 4 green onions, sliced
- 4 cups mixed greens
- 1 roasted red pepper, chopped
- Sea salt to taste

Cajun Shrimp:

- 2 strips bacon, sliced
- 2 teaspoons Cajun seasoning
- 1/2 lb. shrimp, peeled and deveined
- Salt to taste

Preparation:

1. Grate the cauliflower in a food processor.
2. Sauté cauliflower with avocado oil in a skillet for 2 minutes.
3. Stir in coconut milk, cover and cook for 10 minutes on low heat.
4. Mix tapioca starch with water and salt in a bowl and add to the cauliflower.
5. Cook the mixture until creamy with occasional stirring.
6. Sauté greens with oil, green onions, red pepper flakes and salt in a skillet for 3 minutes then transfer to a plate.
7. Sauté bacon in a skillet until crispy then add shrimp, Cajun seasoning, green onions and salt.
8. Sauté for 3 minutes then add ¼ cup water.
9. Cook for 2 minutes then serve the shrimp with greens and cauliflower grits.
10. Enjoy.

Serving Suggestion: Serve the shrimp with lemon slices on top.

Variation Tip: Use white pepper for a change of flavor.

Nutritional Information Per Serving:

Calories 378 | Fat 21g |Sodium 146mg | Carbs 7.1g | Fiber 0.1g | Sugar 0.4g | Protein 23g

Salmon with Cherry Tomatoes

Prep Time: 15 minutes.
Cook Time: 31 minutes.
Serves: 4

Ingredients:

- 1 cup sweet onion, chopped
- 2 teaspoons garlic, minced
- 2 cups cherry tomatoes, halved
- Salt and black pepper, to taste
- 1 ½ tablespoon balsamic vinegar
- 1 1/2 tablespoon basil leaves, julienned
- 1 (2-lbs.) salmon fillet, cut into 4 pieces

Preparation:

1. At 425 degrees F, preheat your oven.
2. Sauté onion with 3 tablespoons olive oil in a sauté pan for 5 minutes.
3. Stir in garlic then sauté for 1 minute.
4. Add ½ teaspoons black pepper, 1 teaspoon salt and tomatoes then cook for 15 minutes with occasional stirring.
5. Stir in basil and vinegar then mix well.
6. Sear the salmon with olive oil in a skillet for 5 minutes per side.
7. Add the tomato mixture on top of the salmon.
8. Serve warm.

Serving Suggestion: Serve the salmon with fresh greens.

Variation Tip: Drizzle cheddar cheese on top for a rich taste.

Nutritional Information Per Serving:
Calories 351 | Fat 4g |Sodium 236mg | Carbs 19.1g | Fiber 0.3g | Sugar 0.1g | Protein 36g

Zucchini Shrimp Scampi

Prep Time: 15 minutes.
Cook Time: 5 minutes.
Serves: 4

Ingredients:

- 2 tablespoons unsalted butter
- 1 lb. shrimp, peeled and deveined
- 3 garlic cloves, minced
- 1/2 teaspoon red pepper flakes
- 1/4 cup chicken stock
- Juice of 1 lemon
- Salt and black pepper, to taste
- 1 1/2 lbs. zucchini, spiralized
- 2 tablespoons Parmesan, grated
- 2 tablespoons parsley leaves, chopped

Preparation:

1. Sauté shrimp with butter, garlic and red pepper flakes in a skillet for 3 minutes.
2. Add chicken stock, black pepper, salt, and lemon juice.
3. Cook to a simmer, add zucchini noodles and cook for 2 minutes.
4. Garnish with parsley and parmesan.
5. Serve warm.

Serving Suggestion: Serve the shrimp zucchini scampi with sweet potato salad.

Variation Tip: Add some chopped bell pepper to the meal.

Nutritional Information Per Serving:
Calories 378 | Fat 7g |Sodium 316mg | Carbs 16.2g | Fiber 0.3g | Sugar 0.3g | Protein 26g

Lemon White Fish Fillets

Prep Time: 15 minutes.
Cook Time: 10 minutes.
Serves: 2

Ingredients:

- 16 ounces cod fillets halibut
- 3 tablespoons olive oil
- 1/4 teaspoon kosher salt
- 1/4 teaspoon black pepper
- 2 lemons, cut in halves

Preparation:

1. Rub the cod fillets with oil, black pepper and oil in a skillet.
2. Cook this codfish for 2 minutes per side.
3. Drizzle lemon juice on top and cook for 3 minutes per side.
4. Enjoy.

Serving Suggestion: Serve the fish with roasted broccoli florets.

Variation Tip: Drizzle lemon zest on top before cooking.

Nutritional Information Per Serving:
Calories 415 | Fat 15g |Sodium 634mg | Carbs 14.3g | Fiber 1.4g | Sugar 1g | Protein 23.3g

Salmon with Herb Garlic Sauce

Prep Time: 15 minutes.
Cook Time: 15 minutes.
Serves: 4

Ingredients:

For the sauce

- 2 garlic cloves, grated
- 3 tablespoons parsley, chopped
- Zest of 1/2 lemon
- Juice of 1/2 lemon
- 3 tablespoons olive oil
- 1/2 teaspoon sea salt

Rest

- 1 tablespoon coconut oil
- 4 salmon fillets
- 12 Brussels sprouts, halved
- 14 asparagus spear, ends cut off
- 1 bunch of broccolini florets
- Olive oil, sea salt, black pepper and lemon

Preparation:

1. At 400 degrees F, preheat your oven.
2. Mix garlic with parsley, lemon juice and zest, and salt in a bowl.
3. Grease a large roast pan with olive oil and set the salmon in it.
4. Spread the lemon juice mixture on top of the salmon.
5. Add the veggies around the salmon and drizzle lemon juice, black pepper and salt on top.
6. Bake the prepared salmon for 15 minutes in the oven.
7. Serve warm.

Serving Suggestion: Serve these fish with toasted bread slices.

Variation Tip: Add garlic salt to the seasoning for more taste.

Nutritional Information Per Serving:

Calories 251 | Fat 17g |Sodium 723mg | Carbs 21g | Fiber 2.5g | Sugar 2g | Protein 7.3g

Baked Lemon Garlic Cod

Prep Time: 15 minutes.
Cook Time: 15 minutes.
Serves: 4

Ingredients:

- 4 (6-ounce) boneless cod fillets
- Sea salt, to taste
- Black pepper, to taste
- 1 1/2 teaspoon unsalted butter
- 1 tablespoon olive oil
- 2 garlic cloves, crushed
- 2 tablespoons lemon juice
- 2 tablespoons parsley, chopped

Preparation:

1. At 400 degrees F, preheat your oven.

2. Grease a baking sheet with cooking oil.
3. Rub the cod pieces with black pepper and salt.
4. Sauté garlic with butter in a skillet for 1 minute.
5. Stir in lemon juice and parsley then mix well.
6. Place the cod pieces in the baking sheet and top them with a garlic mixture.
7. Bake the fish for 14 minutes in the oven.
8. Serve warm.

Serving Suggestion: Serve the fish with roasted broccoli florets.

Variation Tip: Add olives or sliced mushrooms around the fish.

Nutritional Information Per Serving:
Calories 246 | Fat 15g |Sodium 220mg | Carbs 40.3g | Fiber 2.4g | Sugar 1.2g | Protein 12.4g

Zucchini Ravioli

Prep Time: 20 minutes.
Cook Time: 30 minutes.
Serves: 6
Ingredients:

- 1 1/4 lbs. zucchini
- 1 cup part-skim ricotta
- 1/4 cup parmesan
- 1 egg
- 1/4 cup fresh spinach, chopped
- 2 tablespoons fresh basil, chopped
- 1/4 teaspoon nutmeg
- 1/4 teaspoon salt
- 1/8 teaspoons black pepper
- 1 1/2 cups jarred marinara sauce
- 2/3 cup mozzarella, shredded
- 2 tablespoons parmesan, shredded
- 2 teaspoons olive oil
- 1/2 teaspoon black pepper
- Fresh basil, to garnish

Preparation:

1. At 375 degrees F, preheat your oven.
2. Cut the whole zucchini into thin strips using a potato peeler to get 60 slices.
3. Mix black pepper, spinach, egg, salt, nutmeg, basil, spinach, parmesan and ricotta in a bowl.
4. Spread marinara sauce in a 9x13 inches baking dish.
5. Place two zucchini slices on a working surface in a cross.
6. Add a tablespoon filling at the centre of this cross and wrap the zucchini slices around.
7. Place the wraps in the casserole dish and drizzle olive oil, black pepper, salt and remaining cheese on top.
8. Bake the ravioli for 30 minutes in the preheated oven.
9. Serve warm.

Serving Suggestion: Serve the ravioli with pita bread and chili sauce.

Variation Tip: Add mashed sweet potatoes to the filling.

Nutritional Information Per Serving:
Calories 338 | Fat 24g |Sodium 620mg | Carbs 58.3g | Fiber 2.4g | Sugar 1.2g | Protein 5.4g

Cauliflower Salad

Prep Time: 5 minutes.
Cook Time: 0 minutes.
Serves: 4

Ingredients:

- 4 cups cauliflower florets
- 1 tablespoon Tuscan fantasy seasoning
- 1/4 cup apple cider vinegar

Preparation:

1. Toss cauliflower with seasoning and apple cider vinegar in a bowl.
2. Serve.

Serving Suggestion: Serve the cauliflower salad with lemon wedges.

Variation Tip: Add chopped mushrooms and bell pepper to the salad as well.

Nutritional Information Per Serving:
Calories 93 | Fat 3g |Sodium 510mg | Carbs 12g | Fiber 3g | Sugar 4g | Protein 4g

Tofu Spinach Sauté

Prep Time: 10 minutes.
Cook Time: 10 minutes.
Serves: 4

Ingredients:

- 1/4 cup onion, chopped
- 1/4 cup button mushrooms, chopped
- 8 ounces tofu, pressed and chopped
- 3 teaspoons nutritional yeast
- 1 teaspoon liquid aminos
- 4 cups baby spinach
- 4 grape tomatoes, chopped
- Cooking spray

Preparation:

1. Sauté mushrooms and onion with oil in a skillet for 3 minutes.
2. Stir in tofu and sauté for 3 minutes.
3. Add liquid aminos and yeast then mix well.
4. Stir in tomatoes and spinach then sauté for 4 minutes.
5. Serve warm.

Serving Suggestion: Serve the tofu with kale salad.

Variation Tip: Add boiled couscous to the mixture.

Nutritional Information Per Serving:
Calories 378 | Fat 3.8g |Sodium 620mg | Carbs 13.3g | Fiber 2.4g | Sugar 1.2g | Protein 5.4g

Zucchini Lasagna

Prep Time: 15 minutes.
Cook Time: 24 minutes.
Serves: 4

Ingredients:

- 6 ounces crumbled tofu
- 1 garlic clove, minced
- 1 tablespoon dried parsley flakes
- 1 tablespoon dried basil
- 1/8 teaspoons salt
- 1 can diced tomatoes, drained
- 3/4 cup 1% cottage cheese, shredded
- 3 ounces mozzarella cheese, shredded
- 1 tablespoon dried parsley flakes
- 2 tablespoons egg, beaten
- 2 small zucchini squash

Preparation:

1. At 350 degrees F, preheat your oven.
2. Cut the whole zucchini into thin slices using a potato peeler.
3. Sauté tofu with garlic, parsley, basil, and salt in a cooking pan until golden brown.
4. Stir in tomatoes, egg and parsley then cook for 4 minutes.
5. Spread a layer of thin zucchini slices at the bottom of a casserole dish.
6. Top these slices with half of the tofu mixture.
7. Mix cottage cheese with mozzarella cheese in bowl.
8. Drizzle 1/3 of the cheese mixture over the tofu filling.
9. Repeat the zucchini layer and top it with the remaining tofu mixture.
10. Add 1/3 of the cheese mixture and add another layer of zucchini on top.
11. Drizzle remaining cheese on top and bake for 20 minutes in the oven,
12. Serve warm.

Serving Suggestion: Serve the lasagna with the spinach salad.

Variation Tip: Add crispy fried onion on top for better taste.

Nutritional Information Per Serving:
Calories 304 | Fat 31g |Sodium 834mg | Carbs 21.4g | Fiber 0.2g | Sugar 0.3g | Protein 4.6g

Vegetable and Egg Casserole

Prep Time: 15 minutes.
Cook Time: 30 minutes.
Serves: 6

Ingredients:

- 6 eggs
- 1 cup egg whites
- 1 ¼ cup cheese, shredded
- 16 ounces bag frozen spinach
- 2 cups mushrooms, sliced
- 1 bell pepper, diced

Preparation:

1. At 350 degrees F, preheat your oven.

2. Beat egg with egg whites, cheese, spinach, mushrooms and bell pepper in a bowl.
3. Spread this egg mixture into a casserole dish.
4. Bake this casserole for 30 minutes in the oven.
5. Serve warm.

Serving Suggestion: Serve the casserole with cauliflower salad.

Variation Tip: Top the casserole with onion slices before cooking.

Nutritional Information Per Serving:
Calories 341 | Fat 24g |Sodium 547mg | Carbs 36.4g | Fiber 1.2g | Sugar 1g | Protein 10.3g

Green Buddha Bowl

Prep Time: 15 minutes.
Cook Time: 0 minutes.
Serves: 2

Ingredients:

- 1 tablespoon olive oil
- 1 lb brussels sprouts, trimmed and halved
- Salt and black pepper, to taste
- 2 cups cooked quinoa
- 1 cup red apple, chopped
- ¼ cup pepitas
- 1 avocado, sliced
- 1 ½ cups arugula
- ½ cup of mayo
- ¾ cup plain Greek yogurt
- 1 teaspoon ground mustard
- ¼ cup Pompeian White Balsamic Vinegar
- ½ teaspoon salt
- 1 tablespoon fresh basil, chopped
- 1 garlic clove, minced

Preparation:

1. Mix quinoa with apple and the rest of the ingredients in a salad bowl.
2. Serve.

Serving Suggestion: Serve the bowl with spaghetti squash.

Variation Tip: Add some edamame beans to the bowl.

Nutritional Information Per Serving:
Calories 318 | Fat 15.7g |Sodium 124mg | Carbs 27g | Fiber 0.1g | Sugar 0.3g | Protein 4.9g

Lean Mean Soup

Prep Time: 15 minutes.
Cook Time: 30 minutes.
Serves: 6

Ingredients:

- 1/2 head cabbage, chopped
- 3 cups broccoli, chopped
- 1 cup carrots, diced
- 8 stalks celery, diced
- 1 cup onion, diced

- 1 cup radishes, chopped
- 1/2 cup yellow pepper, diced
- 1/2 cup red pepper, diced
- 1/2 cup orange pepper, diced
- 2 tablespoons garlic, minced
- 1 -6 ounce can tomato paste
- 2 -14-ounce cans diced tomatoes with green chiles, undrained
- 6 1/2 cups water
- 1 teaspoon dried parsley
- 1 teaspoon dried oregano
- 1 teaspoon turmeric
- 1/2 cup kale
- Salt and black pepper, to taste

Preparation:

1. Add all the green soup ingredients to a cooking pot.
2. Cook for 30 minutes on low heat until veggies are soft.
3. Serve warm.

Serving Suggestion: Serve the soup with cauliflower rice.

Variation Tip: Add broccoli florets to the soup as well.

Nutritional Information Per Serving:
Calories 114 | Fat 2.2g |Sodium 276mg | Carbs 27.7g | Fiber 0.9g | Sugar 1.4g | Protein 8.8g

Spaghetti Squash

Prep Time: 15 minutes.
Cook Time: 45 minutes.
Serves: 4

Ingredients:

- 1 spaghetti squash
- 1 pinch black pepper
- 1 tablespoon olive oil
- 1 tablespoon Pecorino Romano, shredded

Preparation:

1. At 425 degrees F, preheat your oven.
2. Cut the spaghetti squash in half, remove its seeds and place in a baking sheet.
3. Drizzle black pepper, and olive oil on top, then bake for 45 minutes.
4. Scrap the squash flesh with a fork and add to the serving plate.
5. Drizzle pecorino Romano on top.
6. Serve.

Serving Suggestion: Serve the squash with roasted mushrooms.

Variation Tip: Add lemon zest and lemon juice for better taste.

Nutritional Information Per Serving:
Calories 324 | Fat 5g |Sodium 432mg | Carbs 13.1g | Fiber 0.3g | Sugar 1g | Protein 5.7g

Roasted Green Beans and Mushrooms

Prep Time: 15 minutes.
Cook Time: 25 minutes.
Serves: 4

Ingredients:

- 8 ounces mushrooms, cleaned and halved
- 1 lb. green beans, halved
- 8 whole garlic cloves, halved
- 2 tablespoons olive oil
- 1 tablespoon balsamic vinegar
- Salt and black pepper, to taste

Preparation:

1. At 450 degrees F, preheat your oven.
2. Spread a foil sheet in a baking tray.
3. Add mushrooms, garlic and green beans to the baking sheet.
4. Mix balsamic vinegar with olive oil in a small bowl and pour over the veggies.
5. Drizzle black pepper and salt on top then bake for 25 minutes.
6. Serve warm.

Serving Suggestion: Serve the veggies with toasted bread slices.

Variation Tip: Add boiled zucchini pasta to the mixture.

Nutritional Information Per Serving:
Calories 136 | Fat 10g |Sodium 249mg | Carbs 8g | Fiber 2g | Sugar 3g | Protein 4g

Mexican Cauliflower Rice

Prep Time: 15 minutes.
Cook Time: 14 minutes.
Serves: 4

Ingredients:

- 1 head cauliflower, riced
- 1 tablespoon olive oil
- 1 medium white onion, diced
- 2 garlic cloves, minced
- 1 jalapeno, seeded and minced
- 3 tablespoons tomato paste
- 1 teaspoon of sea salt
- 1 teaspoon cumin
- 1/2 teaspoon paprika
- 3 tablespoons fresh cilantro, chopped
- 1 tablespoon lime juice

Preparation:

1. Grate the cauliflower in a food processor.
2. Sauté onion with oil in a skillet over medium-high heat for 6 minutes.
3. Stir in jalapeno and garlic, then sauté for 2 minutes.
4. Add paprika, cumin, salt, and tomato paste, then sauté for 1 minute.
5. Stir in cauliflower rice and the rest of the ingredients and cook for 5 minutes.
6. Add cilantro and lime juice in the top.
7. Serve.

Serving Suggestion: Serve the rice with roasted veggies on the side.

Variation Tip: Add canned corn to the rice.

Nutritional Information Per Serving:
Calories 351 | Fat 19g |Sodium 412mg | Carbs 43g | Fiber 0.3g | Sugar 1g | Protein 23g

Sheet Pan Chicken

Prep Time: 15 minutes.
Cook Time: 18 minutes.
Serves: 4

Ingredients:

- 1 ¾ pounds boneless chicken breasts, diced
- Salt, to taste
- 1 pound broccoli crowns
- 1 medium red bell pepper
- 2 tablespoons olive oil
- ¼ cup peanut butter
- 1 tablespoon tamari
- 1 tablespoon rice vinegar
- 1 tablespoon honey
- juice from ½ lime
- 3 tablespoons water
- 1 pinch of salt
- Sesame seeds
- Sliced green onions

Preparation:

1. At 425 degrees F, preheat your oven.
2. Layer 2 baking sheets with wax paper and grease with cooking spray.
3. Toss chicken, veggies and all the ingredients in a large bowl.
4. Divide this mixture in the prepared baking seet.
5. Bake the mixture for 18 minutes in the oven.
6. Garnis whti sesame seeds and green onions.
7. Serve warm.

Serving Suggestion: Serve the chicken with a kale salad on the side.

Variation Tip: Coat the chicken with coconut shreds for a crispy texture.

Nutritional Information Per Serving:
Calories 384 | Fat 15g |Sodium 587mg | Carbs 8g | Fiber 1g | Sugar 5g | Protein 20g

Green Chicken Casserole

Prep Time: 15 minutes.
Cook Time: 25 minutes.
Serves: 6

Ingredients:

- 6 whole wheat tortillas
- 1 (15-oz) can white beans
- 1 (12-oz) bag cheese mexican blend, shredded
- 1 cup monterey jack cheese, shredded
- 1 (24-oz) jar salsa verde
- 2 (4-oz) cans of green hatch chiles

- 1 cup shredded salsa chicken
- 1 tablespoon dried oregano

TOPPINGS

- Greek Yogurt
- Guacamole
- Hot sauce
- Fresh cilantro

Preparation:

1. At 375 degrees F, preheat your oven.
2. Spread four tortilla halves in a 9x13 inches baking dish.
3. Top the tortillas with salsa verde to cover.
4. Mix beans with chile mixture and chicken in a bowl.
5. Sprread half of this mixture over the salsa verde.
6. Repeat the layers and top with cheese.
7. Bake for 25 mminutes in the oven at 375 degrees F.
8. Serve warm.

Serving Suggestion: Serve the casserole with roasted green beans.

Variation Tip: Add some sliced onion and spring onion to the casserole.

Nutritional Information Per Serving:

Calories 335 | Fat 5g |Sodium 422mg | Carbs 16g | Fiber 0g | Sugar 1g | Protein 25g

Broccoli Chicken Casserole

Prep Time: 15 minutes.
Cook Time: 20 minutes.
Serves: 4

Ingredients:

- 2 pounds boneless chicken breasts
- 1 tablespoon olive oil
- 2 10-ounce bags frozen cauliflower rice
- 1 (16-ounce) bag frozen broccoli cuts
- 2 large eggs, whisked
- 3 cups mozzarella cheese, shredded
- 2 teaspoons salt
- 2 teaspoons garlic powder
- 2 teaspoons onion powder
- 2 tablespoons butter, melted
- 1 cup Italian blend cheese, shredded

Preparation:

1. At 400 degrees F, preheat your oven.
2. Grease a baking dish with cooking spray.
3. Rub the chicken with oil, black pepper and salt then place in the baking sheet.
4. Bake the chicken breasts for 20 minutes.
5. Cook the cauliflower rice and broccoli as per the package's instructions.
6. Cut the baked chicken into cubes.
7. Mix chicken with rest of the ingredients in a bowl.
8. Spread this mixture in the baking dish and bake for 50 minutes in the oven.
9. Serve warm.

Serving Suggestion: Serve the casserole with roasted veggies.

Variation Tip: Add chopped carrots to the casserole.

Nutritional Information Per Serving:

Calories 369 | Fat 14g |Sodium 442mg | Carbs 13.3g | Fiber 0.4g | Sugar 2g | Protein 32.3g

Chicken with Green Beans

Prep Time: 15 minutes.
Cook Time: 11 minutes.
Serves: 4

Ingredients:

- 1 pound chicken breast cutlets
- 1 teaspoon salt, divided
- ½ teaspoon black pepper
- 2 tablespoons olive oil
- 6 cups green beans, trimmed
- 4 garlic cloves, sliced
- 1 teaspoon lemon zest, grated
- 1 teaspoon fresh thyme, chopped
- ¼ cup chicken broth
- ¼ cup dry white wine
- 1 tablespoon lemon juice
- ¼ cup pine nuts, toasted
- Lemon wedges for garnish

Preparation:

1. Season the chicken with black pepper, oil and salt.
2. Sear the chicken cutlets for 4 minutes per side in a skillet.
3. Sautte green beans with salt, oil and black pepper in a pan for 2 minutes.
4. Stir in wine, broth a nd lemon juie.
5. Cook for 1 minute then add chicken.
6. Garnish with pine nuts, lemon wedges and thyme.
7. Serve warm.

Serving Suggestion: Serve the chicken with fresh cucumber and couscous salad.

Variation Tip: Add some green peas to the mixture.

Nutritional Information Per Serving:

Calories 453 | Fat 2.4g |Sodium 216mg | Carbs 18g | Fiber 2.3g | Sugar 1.2g | Protein 23.2g

Chicken with Avocado Salsa

Prep Time: 15 minutes.
Cook Time: 42 minutes.
Serves: 2

Ingredients:

- 1 ½ pounds boneless chicken breasts

Marinade

- 2 garlic cloves, minced
- 3 tablespoons olive oil
- ¼ cup cilantro, chopped
- Juice of 1 lime

- ½ teaspoons salt
- ¼ teaspoons black pepper

Avocado Salsa

- 2 avocados, diced
- 2 small tomato, chopped
- ¼ cup red onion, chopped
- 1 jalapeno, deseeded and chopped
- 1/4 cup cilantro, chopped
- Juice of 1 lime
- Black pepper and salt to taste

Preparation:

1. Mix all the marinade ingredients in a bowl.
2. Pound and flatten each chicken breast into ¼ inch thickness.
3. Add this chicken to the marinade, mix well, cover and refrigerate for 30 minutes.
4. Grill the chicken for 6 minutes per side in a preheated grill.
5. Serve the chicken with the avocado salsa.
6. Mix all the avocado salsa ingredients in a bowl.
7. Enjoy.

Serving Suggestion: Serve the chicken with cauliflower rice.

Variation Tip: Add dried herbs to the mixture for seasoning.

Nutritional Information Per Serving:
Calories 331 | Fat 20g |Sodium 941mg | Carbs 30g | Fiber 0.9g | Sugar 1.4g | Protein 24.6g

Cheddar Turkey Burgers

Prep Time: 15 minutes.
Cook Time: 14 minutes.
Serves: 4

Ingredients:

- 1 lb lean ground turkey
- 1 (1 ounce) envelope dry ranch dressing
- 1 cup cheddar cheese, shredded
- 1/4 cup green onion, chopped

Preparation:

1. Mix turkey ground with ranch dressing, cheese and green onion in a bowl.
2. Make six patties out of this mixture.
3. Sear each patty in a skillet for 7 minutes per side.
4. Serve warm.

Serving Suggestion: Serve the burgers with fresh herbs on top.

Variation Tip: Add some chopped bell pepper to the patties.

Nutritional Information Per Serving:
Calories 332 | Fat 18g |Sodium 611mg | Carbs 13.3g | Fiber 0g | Sugar g4 | Protein 38g

Turkey Taco Soup

Prep Time: 15 minutes.
Cook Time: 45 minutes.
Serves: 6
Ingredients:

- 1 ½ lbs. lean ground turkey
- 1 onion, diced
- 1 (1 ¼ ounces) package taco seasoning
- 1 (1 ounce) package ranch dressing seasoning
- 1 (14oz) can chicken broth
- 1 (4 ounces) can diced green chiles
- 1 (15 ½ ounces) can whole kernel corn
- 1 (15 ½ ounces)can pinto beans
- 1 (15 ounces) can refried beans
- 1 (14 ½ ounces) can diced tomatoes with green chiles
- 1 (14 ½ ounces) can mexican diced tomatoes

Preparation:

1. Saute onion and turkey in a skillet until golden brown.
2. Stir in rest of the ingredients and cook for 45 minutes.
3. Serve warm.

Serving Suggestion: Serve the soup with toasted bread slices.

Variation Tip: Add zucchini noodles to the soup.

Nutritional Information Per Serving:
Calories 354 | Fat 25g |Sodium 412mg | Carbs 22.3g | Fiber 0.2g | Sugar 1g | Protein 28.3g

Chicken Zucchini

Prep Time: 15 minutes.
Cook Time: 30 minutes.

Serves: 4
Ingredients:

- 4 pieces of chicken breast
- 1 cup Zucchini, chopped
- 2 tablespoons shredded cheese
- 1 raw onion, chopped
- Salt, to taste
- Black pepper, to taste
- Oregano, to taste

Preparation:

1. At 450 degrees F, preheat your oven.
2. Place the chicken breast in a baking pan and drizzle oregano, black pepper and salt on top.
3. Drizzle cheese on top and cover the chicken with zucchini slices.
4. Bake this chicken for 30 minutes in the oven.
5. Serve warm.

Serving Suggestion: Serve the chicken with white rice or sweet potato salad.

Variation Tip: Add some zucchini noodles to the chicken.

Nutritional Information Per Serving:
Calories 405 | Fat 15g |Sodium 852mg | Carbs 7g | Fiber 2g | Sugar 2g | Protein 15g

Turkey Shepherd's Pie

Prep Time: 15 minutes.
Cook Time: 30 minutes.
Serves: 4

Ingredients:

- 12 ounces lean ground turkey
- 2 cups cooked potatoes, mashed
- 1 cup frozen corn
- 1/2 cup tomatoes, diced
- 1/2 cup carrots, diced
- 1/2 cup zucchini, diced
- 1/4 cup onions, chopped
- 3 teaspoons garlic, minced
- salt and black pepper, to taste

Preparation:

1. Sauté turkey with black pepper, salt, garlic, carrots, and onion in a skillet until golden brown.
2. Spread the turkey in a 9x12 inch baking pan.
3. Top it with tomatoes, zucchini, carrots, garlic and onion.
4. Add frozen corn and mashed potatoes on top.
5. Bake this casserole for 20 minutes in the oven at 350 degrees F.
6. Serve warm.

Serving Suggestion: Serve the pie with avocado tomato salad.

Variation Tip: Add boiled peas to the pie.

Nutritional Information Per Serving:
Calories 352 | Fat 14g |Sodium 220mg | Carbs 16g | Fiber 0.2g | Sugar 1g | Protein 26g

Sesame Chicken

Prep Time: 15 minutes.
Cook Time: 20 minutes.
Serves: 2

Ingredients:

- 1 lb boneless chicken breasts, diced
- 1 large head of broccoli, chopped
- 2 red bell peppers, cut into chunks
- 1 cup snap peas
- Salt and black pepper, to taste
- Sesame seeds and green onions

Sauce:

- 1/4 cup soy sauce
- 1 tablespoon sweet chili sauce
- 2 tablespoons honey
- 2 garlic cloves
- 1 teaspoon fresh ginger

Preparation:

1. At 400 degrees F, preheat your oven.
2. Mix all the sauce ingredients in a saucepan and cook until it thickens.
3. Remove the sauce from the heat and allow the sauce to cool.
4. Spread the veggies and chicken in a greased baking sheet.
5. Drizzle sauce over the mixture and mix well.
6. Bake the mixture for 20 minutes in the oven.
7. Garnish with sesame seeds.
8. Serve warm.

Serving Suggestion: Serve the chicken with toasted bread on the side.

Variation Tip: Add some canned corn to the meal.

Nutritional Information Per Serving:
Calories 334 | Fat 16g |Sodium 462mg | Carbs 31g | Fiber 0.4g | Sugar 3g | Protein 25.3g

Turkey Broccoli

Prep Time: 15 minutes.
Cook Time: 20 minutes.
Serves: 4

Ingredients:

- 1 tablesepoon Dijon mustard
- 1 tablespoon whole grain mustard
- 1 cup chicken broth
- 4 teaspoons roasted garlic oil
- 4 cups broccoli florets
- 1 tablespoon garlic gusto seasoning
- 1½ lb boneless turkey breasts, diced
- 1 pinch dash of desperation seasoning

Preparation:

1. Mix broth with mustard in a bowl.
2. Saute broccoli with oil and garlic gusto in a skillet for 2 minutes.
3. Transfer the broccoli to a bowl.
4. Sear the turkey bites in the same pan for 5 minutes per side.
5. Reduce heat, and stir in mustard mixture and broccoli.
6. Cover and cook for 7 minutes on a simmer.
7. Serve warm.

Serving Suggestion: Serve the chicken with a spinach salad.

Variation Tip: Add chopped green beans to the mixture.

Nutritional Information Per Serving:
Calories 388 | Fat 8g |Sodium 339mg | Carbs 8g | Fiber 1g | Sugar 2g | Protein 33g

Chicken Piccata

Prep Time: 15 minutes.
Cook Time: 10 minutes.
Serves: 8
Ingredients:

- 8 boneless chicken breast halves
- 3 teaspoons olive oil
- 2 tablespoons butter
- 1/2 cup all-purpose flour

- 1/2 cup Parmesan cheese, grated
- 1/2 cup egg
- 1/2 teaspoon salt
- 2 tablespoons 1/4 cup dry white wine
- 1/4 cup parsley minced
- 1/8 teaspoon hot pepper sauce
- 5 tablespoons lemon juice
- 3 garlic cloves, minced

Preparation:

1. Pound and flatten each chicken piece.
2. Beat egg with hot pepper sauce, garlic, and 2 tablespoons lemon juice in a bowl.
3. Mix flour with salt, parsley, and Parmesan cheese in a bowl.
4. First coat the chicken with the flour mixture then dip in the egg mixture and coat again with the flour mixture.
5. Place the coated chicken a greased skillet and cook for 5 minutes per side.
6. Mix lemon juice, melted butter and remaining wine in a saucepan and boil.
7. Drizzle this sauce over the chicken.
8. Serve warm.

Serving Suggestion: Serve the chicken with a fresh crouton's salad.

Variation Tip: Add a drizzle of cheese on top.

Nutritional Information Per Serving:
Calories 300 | Fat 2g |Sodium 374mg | Carbs 30g | Fiber 6g | Sugar 3g | Protein 32g

Baked Chicken Stuffed

Prep Time: 15 minutes.
Cook Time: 22 minutes.
Serves: 4
Ingredients:

- 4 chicken breast halves
- 4 ounces baby bella mushrooms
- 1/4 cup onion, chopped
- 1/2 teaspoon ground thyme
- 1/2 teaspoon salt
- 1/4 cup mozzarella cheese, shredded

Preparation:

1. At 350 degrees F, preheat your oven.
2. Layer a 9x13 inches baking dish with cooking oil.
3. Saute mushrooms, onions, salt and thyme in a skillet for 7 minutes.
4. Make a pocket in each chiekn breast and stuff each with the msurhoos mixture and cheese.
5. Place these chicken pockets in the baking dish.
6. Bake for 15 minutes in the oven.
7. Serve warm.

Serving Suggestion: Serve the chicken with steaming white rice.

Variation Tip: Add roasted peanuts on top.

Nutritional Information Per Serving:
Calories 301 | Fat 16g |Sodium 189mg | Carbs 32g | Fiber 0.3g | Sugar 0.1g | Protein 28.2g

Spinach Mushroom Chicken

Prep Time: 15 minutes.
Cook Time: 43 minutes.
Serves: 4

Ingredients:

- 6 ounces bag raw spinach leaves
- 2 ounces cream cheese
- 2 garlic cloves, minced
- 8 ounces baby bella mushrooms
- 2 teaspoons garlic powder
- 2 teaspoons salt
- 2 teaspoons ground thyme
- 4 chicken breasts
- 4 mozzarella cheese slices

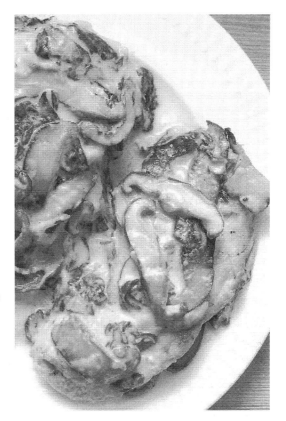

Preparation:

1. At 400 degrees F, preheat your oven.
2. Season chicken with thyme, salt and 1 teaspoon garlic powder.
3. Place this chicken in a casserole dish and bake for 15 minutes in the oven.
4. Saute garlic in a skillet for 1 minute.
5. Stir in spinach and cook for 10 minutes.
6. Add cream cheese then mix well and remove from the heat.
7. Saute mushrooms with thyme, salt, and 1 teaspoon garlic powder in a skillet for 7 minutes.
8. Stir in cream cheese mixture and mix well.
9. Spread this mixture on top of the baked chicken.
10. Drizzle cheese on top and bake another 10 minutes.
11. Serve warm.

Serving Suggestion: Serve the chicken with toasted bread slices.

Variation Tip: Add butter sauce on top of the chicken before cooking.

Nutritional Information Per Serving:

Calories 419 | Fat 13g |Sodium 432mg | Carbs 9.1g | Fiber 3g | Sugar 1g | Protein 21g

Green Lamb Curry

Prep Time: 15 minutes.
Cook Time: 2 hrs. 30 minutes.
Serves: 2

Ingredients:

- 2/3 lb. lean lamb, trimmed and diced
- 2½ tablespoons curry powder
- ½ teaspoons salt
- 1 tablespoon vegetable oil
- 2 onions, sliced
- 4 garlic cloves, chopped
- 1 tablespoon tomato purée
- ½ lb. fresh spinach
- Small bunch of coriander leaves, to serve
- Black pepper, to taste

Preparation:

1. Mix lamb meat with salt, black pepper and curry powder in a bowl.
2. Saute onions with oil in a skillet on medium heat until soft.
3. Stir in lamb and saute until brown.
4. Add garlic, tomato puree and water then cover and cook for 2 hours on medium heat.
5. Remove the lid and cook for 20 minutes.
6. Stir in spinach and cook for 3 minutes.
7. Garnish and serve warm.

Serving Suggestion: Serve the curry with white rice.

Variation Tip: Add some kale leaves instead of the spinach

Nutritional Information Per Serving:
Calories 305 | Fat 25g |Sodium 532mg | Carbs 2.3g | Fiber 0.4g | Sugar 2g | Protein 18.3g

Lamb Pea Curry

Prep Time: 15 minutes.
Cook Time: 22 minutes.
Serves: 2

Ingredients:

- 1 ¼ cups jasmine rice
- Cooking spray oil
- 14 ounces lean lamb medallions
- 5 teaspoons Thai green curry paste
- 1 red onion, sliced
- 14 ounces can creamy coconut evaporated milk
- 2 teaspoons fish sauce
- 1 ½ cups frozen peas
- 14 ounces mix carrot sticks, snow peas, amd broccoli florets

Preparation:

1. Sear the lamb with half of the curry paste and oil in a cooking pan for 2 minutes per side.
2. Cover this lamb and bake for 7 minutes at 400 degrees F.
3. Meanwhile, saute onion with remainig oil and curry paste in a skillet for 1 minute.
4. Stir in fish sauce and milk then cook for 5 minutes.
5. Add vegetables and cook for 5 minutes.
6. Slice the lamb and serve with veggies.
7. Enjoy.

Serving Suggestion: Serve the curry with toasted bread slices.

Variation Tip: Add crumbled feta cheese on top.

Nutritional Information Per Serving:
Calories 325 | Fat 16g |Sodium 431mg | Carbs 22g | Fiber 1.2g | Sugar 4g | Protein 23g

Lemon Lamb Chops

Prep Time: 15 minutes.
Cook Time: 18 minutes.
Serves: 8

Ingredients:

- Zest of 2 lemons
- 1 tablespoon oregano, chopped
- 1 ¼ teaspoons salt
- Black pepper to taste

- 8 lamb loin chops, trimmed
- 1/4 cup tahini
- ¼ cup nonfat yogurt
- ¼ cup seeded cucumber, diced
- ¼ cup lemon juice
- 2 garlic cloves, minced
- 1 tablespoon fresh parsley, chopped
- 3 tablespoons water
- 2 teaspoons olive oil

Preparation:

1. At 400 degrees F, preheat your ove,
2. Rub the lamb chops with black pepper ¾ teaspoons salt, oregano and lemon zest.
3. Cover and refrigerate these lamb chops for 1 hour.
4. Mix tahini with ½ teaspoons salt, parsley, garlic, lemon juice, cucumber and yogurt in a small bowl.
5. Sear lamb chops with oil in a skillet for 2 minutes per side.
6. Now bake them for 14 mintues in the oven.
7. Pour the tahini sauce on top.
8. Serve warm.

Serving Suggestion: Serve these chops with cauliflower rice.

Variation Tip: Add toasted croutons on top.

Nutritional Information Per Serving:
Calories 425 | Fat 14g |Sodium 411mg | Carbs 44g | Fiber 0.3g | Sugar 1g | Protein 28.3g

Braised Lamb Shanks

Prep Time: 15 minutes.
Cook Time: 2 hr. 30 minutes.
Serves: 4

Ingredients:

- 1 ½ pounds eggplant, peeled
- 4 (12-ounce) lamb shanks, trimmed
- 2 tablespoons ground sumac
- 1 ¼ teaspoons salt
- ½ teaspoon black pepper
- 2 tablespoons olive oil
- 1 green bell pepper, diced
- 1 small onion, diced
- 3 garlic cloves, minced
- 5 plum tomatoes, diced
- 1 cup water
- ½ cup parsley, chopped

Preparation:

1. Rub the lamb shanks with black pepper, salt and 1 tablespoon sumac.
2. Sear lamb with 1 tablespoon oil in a large Dutch oven for 5 minutes per side.
3. Transfer the lamb to a plate.
4. Add remaining 1 tablespoon oil, onion, minced garlic cloves, bell pepper and 1 tablespoon sumac.
5. Saute for 5 minutes then return the lamb to the pot.
6. Stir in tomatoes, water and eggplant then cover and cook on a simmer for 2 hours.
7. Remove the lid and cook for 10 minutes until the gravy thickens.
8. Garnish with parsley and serve warm.

Serving Suggestion: Serve the shanks with sweet potato salad.

Variation Tip: Add chopped green onion to the topping.

Nutritional Information Per Serving:
Calories 425 | Fat 15g |Sodium 345mg | Carbs 12.3g | Fiber 1.4g | Sugar 3g | Protein 23.3g

Lamb Cabbage Rolls

Prep Time: 15 minutes.
Cook Time: 1 hr. 10 minutes.
Serves: 8

Ingredients:

- ½ cup bulgur, cooked
- 1 large head Savoy cabbage
- 2 tablespoons olive oil
- 2 cups onion, chopped
- 1 cup leeks, chopped
- ¾ teaspoon salt
- ¾ teaspoon black pepper
- ½ teaspoon ground turmeric
- ¼ teaspoon ground ginger
- ¼ teaspoon ground allspice
- 1 pinch of ground cinnamon
- 12 ounces ground lamb
- ½ cup parsley, chopped
- 2 teaspoons fresh mint, chopped
- 1 large egg, beaten
- ½ cup white wine
- ½ cup chicken broth
- 2 teaspoons lemon zest, grated
- 3 tablespoons lemon juice

Preparation:

1. At 325 degrees F, preheat your oven.
2. Boil cabbage leaves in 2 ½ cups water in a cooking pan and drain.
3. Saute onion and leeks with oil in a skillet for 8 minutes.
4. Add cinnamon, allspice, ginger, turmeric, black pepper and salt then cook for 1 minute.
5. Transfer this mixture to a bowl and add bulgur.
6. Stir in lamb, parsley, mint and egg then mix well.
7. Spread the cabbage leaves o nthe working surface.
8. Divide the lamb filling at the center oeach leave.
9. Wrap the leaves around the filling and place the wrap in a baking dish.
10. Add lemon juice, lemon zest, broth and wine around the cabbage rolls.
11. Cover the dish with a foil sheet and bake for 1 hour in the oven.
12. Serve warm.

Serving Suggestion: Serve the rolls with roasted asparagus.

Variation Tip: Add a drizzle of parmesan cheese on top.

Nutritional Information Per Serving:
Calories 391 | Fat 5g |Sodium 88mg | Carbs 3g | Fiber 0g | Sugar 0g | Protein 27g

Pork with Caramelized Mushrooms

Prep Time: 15 minutes.
Cook Time: 20 minutes.
Serves: 2

Ingredients:

- 1 lb. lean ground pork
- 8 ounces mushrooms, sliced
- 1 small onion, sliced
- 1 tablespoon garlic, minced
- 1 tablespoon fresh ginger, grated
- 12 ounces bag whole green beans
- 2 tablespoons olive oil
- 1/4 cup water

SAUCE

- 2 tablespoons soy sauce
- 2 tablespoons mirin
- 1 tablespoon rice vinegar
- 2 teaspoons brown sugar
- 1 teaspoon sriracha
- 1 teaspoon dark sesame oil

Preparation:

1. Mix all the sauce ingredients in a small bowl.
2. Saute mushrooms with 1 tablespoon oil in a skillet until soft.
3. Stir in ground pork and saute until brown.
4. Add remaining oil, garlic, ginger, green beans and onion then saute for 2 minutes.
5. Stir in water and cook for another 2 minutes.
6. Pour in the prepared sauce and cook until the liquid is reduced to half.
7. Serve warm.

Serving Suggestion: Serve the pork with cauliflower rice.

Variation Tip: Add a layer of the boiled zucchini noodles to the stir fry.

Nutritional Information Per Serving:

Calories 376 | Fat 21g |Sodium 476mg | Carbs 12g | Fiber 3g | Sugar 4g | Protein 20g

Pepper Taco Bake

Prep Time: 15 minutes.

Cook Time: 30 minutes.

Serves: 4

Ingredients:

- 1 lb. lean ground beef
- 1 tablespoon Phoenix Sunrise Seasoning
- 1 cup vegetable salsa
- 1 ½ lbs fresh bell peppers, quartered
- 1/2 cup cheddar cheese, shredded
- 4 tablespoons sour cream

Preparation:

1. At 350 degrees F, preheat your oven.
2. Mix ground meat with salsa and seasoning in a large bowl.

3. Divide this mixture in the pepper halves and place these peppers in a baking dish.
4. Drizzle cheese on top and bake for 30 minutes in the oven.
5. Garnish with sour cream cheese and serve warm.

Serving Suggestion: Serve the bake with a fresh greens salad.

Variation Tip: Add chopped herbs on top.

Nutritional Information Per Serving:
Calories 487 | Fat 24g |Sodium 686mg | Carbs 17g | Fiber 1g | Sugar 1.2g | Protein 22g

Pan Seared Beef and Mushrooms

Prep Time: 15 minutes.
Cook Time: 17 minutes.
Serves: 4

Ingredients:

- 1 ½ lbs lean beef, cubed
- 1/2 tablespoon Dash of Desperation Seasoning
- Nonstick cooking spray
- 4 cups mushrooms, sliced
- 1 cup beef broth
- 1 ½ teaspoon Garlic Gusto Seasoning

Preparation:

1. Mix beef with seasoning and saute in a skillet with cooking spray for 7 minutes.
2. Add broth and rest of the ingredients and cook or 10 minutes with occasional stirring.
3. Serve warm.

Serving Suggestion: Serve the beef with sweet potato salad.

Variation Tip: Drizzle parmesan cheese on top before serving.

Nutritional Information Per Serving:
Calories 255 | Fat 12g |Sodium 66mg | Carbs 13g | Fiber 2g | Sugar 4g | Protein 22g

Sirloin with Horseradish Sauce

Prep Time: 15 minutes.
Cook Time: 14 minutes
Serves: 2

Ingredients:

- 1 ½ pounds sirloin steaks
- ½ tablesoon dash of desperation seasoning
- 6 tablespoons sour cream
- 3 tablespoons horseradish

Preparation:

1. At medium high heat heat, preheat your grill.
2. Season the steak with Dash seasoning and grill for 7 minutes per side.
3. Mix rest of the ingredients in a bowl.
4. Slice the grilled steak and pour the sauce over steak.
5. Serve warm.

Serving Suggestion: Serve the sirloin with fresh herbs on top.

Variation Tip: Add butter to the meat before serving.

Nutritional Information Per Serving:
Calories 405 | Fat 22.7g |Sodium 227mg | Carbs 26.1g | Fiber 1.4g | Sugar 0.9g | Protein 35.2g

Chipotle Pork Loin

Prep Time: 15 minutes.
Cook Time: 6 hours.
Serves: 4

Ingredients:

- 2 pounds boneless pork loin
- 1 tablespoon Garlic and Spring Onion Seasoning
- 1 tablespoon Cinnamon Chipotle Seasoning
- ¼ cup water

Preparation:

1. Add pork loin, water, seasoning and chipotle to a slow cooker.
2. Cover and cook for 6 hours on Low heat.
3. Serve warm.

Serving Suggestion: Serve the pork loin with sautéed carrots on the side.

Variation Tip: Drizzle parmesan cheese on top before serving.

Nutritional Information Per Serving:
Calories 345 | Fat 36g |Sodium 272mg | Carbs 41g | Fiber 0.2g | Sugar 0.1g | Protein 22.5g

Cauliflower Ground Beef Hash

Prep Time: 15 minutes.
Cook Time: 25 minutes.
Serves: 4

Ingredients:

- 16 ounces frozen cauliflower
- 1 lb. lean ground beef
- 2 cups cheddar cheese, shredded
- 1 teaspoon garlic powder
- Salt and black pepper to taste

Preparation:

1. Saute beef in a cooking pan until brown.
2. Stir in garlic, salt, black pepper and cauliflower then cook until soft.
3. Stir in cheddar cheese and cook until the cheese is melted.
4. Serve warm.

Serving Suggestion: Serve the beef hash with sautéed green beans and mashed sweet potatoes.

Variation Tip: Drizzle parmesan cheese on top before cooking.

Nutritional Information Per Serving:
Calories 395 | Fat 9.5g |Sodium 655mg | Carbs 13.4g | Fiber 0.4g | Sugar 0.4g | Protein 28.3g

Mojo Marinated Flank Steak

Prep Time: 15 minutes.
Cook Time: 10 minutes.
Serves: 4

Ingredients:

- 2 pounds flank steak
- 2 tablespoons fresh lime juice
- 1 tablespoon garlic Gusto seasoning
- 1 teaspoon ground cumin
- 1/3 cup beef broth
- 1 pinch Dash of Desperation Seasoning

Preparation:

1. Mix beef with remaining ingredients except dash seasoning, in a large bowl.
2. Cover the meat and refrigerate for 1 hour at least.
3. Preheat and grease a grill for cooking.
4. Remove the meat from the marinate and rub with the dash seasoning.
5. Grill the steak for 5 minutes per side.
6. Slice and serve warm.

Serving Suggestion: Serve the steaks with fresh green and mashed sweet potatoes.

Variation Tip: Add zucchini noodles on the side

Nutritional Information Per Serving:

Calories 301 | Fat 5g |Sodium 340mg | Carbs 24.7g | Fiber 1.2g | Sugar 1.3g | Protein 15.3g

Pork Loin with Tomatoes and Olives

Prep Time: 15 minutes.
Cook Time: 6 hours.
Serves: 4

Ingredients:

- 2 lbs pork tenderloin
- 1 cup chicken broth
- 2 teaspoons Garlic Gusto Seasoning
- 1/2 teaspoon Mediterranean Seasoning
- 10 green olives, sliced
- 1 tablespoon sun dried tomatoes, sliced

Preparation:

1. Add ork and all the ingredients to a crock pot and cover to a cook for 6 hours on Low heat.
2. Slice the meat and serve warm.

Serving Suggestion: Serve the pork with roasted green beans.

Variation Tip: Add sliced black kalamata olives to the pork, if needed.

Nutritional Information Per Serving:

Calories 448 | Fat 23g |Sodium 350mg | Carbs 18g | Fiber 6.3g | Sugar 1g | Protein 40.3g

Pork Tenderloins with Mushrooms

Prep Time: 15 minutes.
Cook Time: 32 minutes.
Serves: 6

Ingredients:

- Cooking spray
- 1 teaspoon dash seasoning
- 1 1/2 lbs pork tenderloin
- 6 cups portobello mushrooms, chopped
- 1/2 cup chicken broth
- 1 tablespoon garlic gusto
- Fresh parsley for garnish

Preparation:

1. At 400 degrees F, preheat your oven.
2. Rub the seasoning over the tenderloin.
3. Sear the tenderloin in a skillet, greased with cooking spray, for 3 minutes per side.
4. Trasnfer the seared pork to a plate.
5. Add rest of the ingredients to the same skillet and cook for 1 minute.
6. Return the pork tenderloin to the skillet and bake for 25 minutes.
7. Slice the pork and serve warm.

Serving Suggestion: Serve the pork with toasted bread slices.

Variation Tip: Replace mushrooms with chopped sweet potatoes.

Nutritional Information Per Serving:
Calories 309 | Fat 25g |Sodium 463mg | Cars 9.9g | Fiber 0.3g | Sugar 0.3g | Protein 28g

Herb Roasted Tenderloin

Prep Time: 15 minutes.
Cook Time: 60 minutes.
Serves: 8

Ingredients:

- 4 lbs pork tenderloin, lean
- 2 teaspoons black pepper
- 4 tablespoons parmesan cheese, grated
- 2 tablespoons fresh rosemary
- 1 tablespoon fresh thyme
- 1/2 teaspoon garlic, minced
- 1/2 teaspoon cumin
- 1/8 teaspoon salt
- 1 small onion, sliced
- 1/2 cup water

Preparation:

1. At 350 degrees, preheat your oven.
2. Mix cheese with spices in a bowl and rub over the pork.
3. Spread onion slices in a baking sheet and place the pork on top.
4. Add herbs on top and add ½ cup water around the pork.
5. Bake the pork for 1 hour in the preheated oven.
6. Serve warm.

Serving Suggestion: Serve the pork tenderloin with roasted green beans.

Variation Tip: Add paprika for more spice.

Nutritional Information Per Serving:

Calories 537 | Fat 20g |Sodium 719mg | Carbs 25.1g | Fiber 0.9g | Sugar 1.4g | Protein 37.8g

Shrimp Salad

Prep Time: 15 minutes.
Cook Time: 17 minutes.
Serves: 2

Ingredients:

- 2 tablespoons olive oil
- 1/3 cup red onion, chopped
- 3 cups broccoli slaw
- 3 cups broccoli florets
- 1/2 teaspoon salt
- 2 garlic cloves, minced
- 1/2 pound shrimp, peeled and deveined
- 1 teaspoon lime juice
- Green onions, chopped, for garnish
- Cilantro, chopped
- Sriracha and red pepper flakes, for garnish

Sesame almond dressing:

- 2 tablespoons almond butter
- 2 tablespoons water
- 1 tablespoon sesame oil
- 1 tablespoon tamari
- 1 tablespoon maple syrup
- 1 teaspoon lime juice
- 1 teaspoon ginger, minced
- 1 clove minced garlic
- 1 teaspoon sriracha sauce
- 1/4 teaspoon black pepper

Preparation:

1. Mix all the sesame almond dressing in a bowl.
2. Saute onion with oil in a skillet for 5 minutes.
3. Stir in broccoli slaw and florest then saute for 7 minutes.
4. Add black pepper and salt then transfer to a plate.
5. Add minced garlic, shrimp, lime juice and more oil to the same skillet.
6. Saute for 5 minutes then transfer the shrimp to the broccoli.
7. Pour the sesame dressing on top and garnish with cilantro and green onions.
8. Serve warm.

Serving Suggestion: Serve the shrimp salad with cauliflower rice risotto.

Variation Tip: Add paprika for more spice.

Nutritional Information Per Serving:

Calories 212 | Fat 9g |Sodium 353mg | Carbs 8g | Fiber 3g | Sugar 4g | Protein 25g

Salmon Chowder

Prep Time: 15 minutes.
Cook Time: 20 minutes.
Serves: 6

Ingredients:

- 3 tablespoons olive oil
- 1 onion, diced
- 1 small fennel bulb, diced
- 1 cup celery, sliced
- 4 garlic cloves, chopped
- 1 teaspoon fennel seeds
- 1/2 teaspoon thyme
- 1/2 teaspoon smoked paprika
- 1/3 cup vermouth
- 3 cups fish stock
- 3/4 lb baby potatoes, sliced
- 1 teaspoon salt
- 1 bay leaf
- 1 lb salmon, skinless, diced
- 2 cups almond milk

Preparation:

1. lery, fennel, and onion wit Sauté ceh oil in a skillet for 6 minutes.
2. Stir in thyme, fennel seeds and garlic then saute for 2 minutes.
3. Add smoked paprika and vermouth then cook for 2 minutes.
4. Stir in salt, stock, bay, thyme, and potatoes then cook for 10 minutes on a simmer.
5. Stir in salmon bones, salt and milk then cook for 2 minutes.
6. Garnish with lemon wedges, fennel frongs and dill.
7. Serve warm.

Serving Suggestion: Serve the chowder with zucchini noodles.

Variation Tip: Add mixed chopped herbs and lemon zest to the chowder.

Nutritional Information Per Serving:
Calories 376 | Fat 17g |Sodium 1127mg | Carbs 24g | Fiber 1g | Sugar 3g | Protein 29g

Halibut with Zucchini Noodles

Prep Time: 15 minutes.
Cook Time: 17 minutes.
Serves: 8

Ingredients:

- 8 (10 ounces) halibut
- 1 garlic clove, smashed
- 2 tablespoons olive oil
- Salt and black pepper to taste

Noodles:

- 1 tablespoon olive oil
- 1 shallot, sliced
- 3 garlic cloves, chopped
- 16 ounces zucchini noodles

- Salt and black pepper to taste
- 2 teaspoons lemon zest
- ½ cup Italian parsley, chopped
- 1 tablespoon lemon juice

Preparation:

1. At 375 degrees F, preheat your oven.
2. Saute garlic with oil in a skillet over medium heat for 30 seconds.
3. Rub the black pepper and salt over the fish.
4. Sear this fish in the skillet for 6 minutes per side.
5. Transfer this fish to a plate and keep it aside.
6. Stir zucchini, black pepper and salt then saute for 4 minutes.
7. Stir in parsley, lemon zest and lemon juice.
8. Serve the zucchini noodles with fish on top.
9. Enjoy.

Serving Suggestion: Serve the noodles with fresh greens on the side.

Variation Tip: Roll the fish in breadcrumbs for a crispy touch.

Nutritional Information Per Serving:
Calories 457 | Fat 19g |Sodium 557mg | Carbs 19g | Fiber 1.8g | Sugar 1.2g | Protein 32.5g

Poached Mahi Mahi

Prep Time: 15 minutes.
Cook Time: 31 minutes.
Serves: 4

Ingredients:

- 4 (4-ounces) boneless mahi mahi fillets
- 1/4 teaspoon salt
- 1 cup olive oil
- 1 lb asparagus, trimmed
- 3 tablespoons olive oil
- 1 yellow onion, chopped
- 1/4 teaspoon black pepper
- 1 pinch red pepper glakes
- 10 green olives, pitted and chopped
- 1 small head garlic, minced
- 1 cup jarred roasted red peppers, chopped
- 2 tablespoons capers, drained, chopped
- 1/2 cup dry white wine
- 1/2 cup fresh basil, chopped
- 1 tablespoon fresh lemon juice
- Lemon wedges for serving

Preparation:

1. At 250 degrees F, preheat your oven.
2. Rub the fish with salt and keep it aside.
3. Add oil and fish to a skillet and sear for 3 minutes per side.
4. Bake this for 15 minutes then cover and keep it warm.
5. Saute onions with black pepper, pepper flakes and oil in a skillet for 4 minutes.
6. Stir in red pepper, capers, garlic and olives then cook for 2 minutes.
7. Add wine and cook the mixture for 3 minutes on a simmer.
8. Stir in asparagus tips and cook for 1 minute.

9. Add lemon juice, parsley and basil then over the fish.

10. Garnish with lemon wedges.

11. Serve warm.

Serving Suggestion: Serve the fish with cauliflower rice.

Variation Tip: Replace mahi mahi with codfish if needed.

Nutritional Information Per Serving:

Calories 392 | Fat 16g |Sodium 466mg | Carbs 3.9g | Fiber 0.9g | Sugar 0.6g | Protein 48g

Creamy Scallops

Prep Time: 15 minutes.
Cook Time: 9 minutes.
Serves: 3

Ingredients:

- 2 tablespoons olive oil
- 1 ¼ pounds scallops
- 2 tablespoons unsalted butter
- 5 garlic cloves, minced
- Salt and black pepper to taste
- 1/4 cup dry white wine
- 1 cup heavy cream
- 1 tablespoon lemon juice
- 1/4 cup parsley, chopped

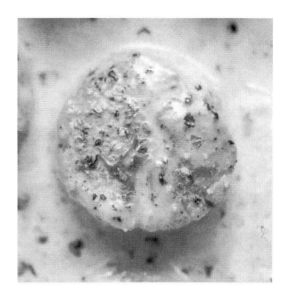

Preparation:

1. Sear the scallops in a skillet with oil for 3 minutes per side.
2. Season them with black pepper and salt then transfer to a plate.
3. Saute garlic with 2 tablespoons butter in a skillet for 1 minute.
4. Stir in wine and cook for 2 minutes then add cream.
5. Cook this mixture until mixture thickens then add lemon juice.
6. Return the scallops to the skillet and garnish with parsley.
7. Serve warm.

Serving Suggestion: Serve the scallops with cauliflower salad.

Variation Tip: Add some cream cheese to the scallops.

Nutritional Information Per Serving:

Calories 316 | Fat 22g |Sodium 356mg | Carbs 7g | Fiber 2.4g | Sugar 5g | Protein 18g

Tuna Broccoli Mornay

Prep Time: 15 minutes.
Cook Time: 30 minutes.
Serves: 4

Ingredients:

- 1 x ½ lb. can Tuna in springwater, drained
- 3 oz. spiral pasta
- 1 head broccoli, florets
- 3 ½ ounce baby spinach leaves, washed
- 1 onion, diced
- 1 ounce butter
- 3 tablespoons flour
- Salt and black pepper, to taste

- 2 cups milk
- 1¼ cup grated cheese
- ¼ cup breadcrumbs

Preparation:

1. At 360 degrees F, preheat your oven.
2. Boil pasta as per the package's instructions then drain and keep it aside.
3. Sauté onion with butter in a cooking pan until sfot.
4. Stir in flour and sauté for 30 seconds.
5. Add milk, mix well and cook until the mixture thickens.
6. Add spinach and cook until the leaves are wilted.
7. Stir in 1 cup grated cheese, broccoli, tuna and black pepper.
8. Spread this mixture in a casserole dish and spread remaining cheese and breadcrumbs on top.
9. Bake for 25 minutes in the preheated oven.
10. Serve warm.

Serving Suggestion: Serve the mornay with sautéed vegetables.

Variation Tip: Add canned corn to the mornay.

Nutritional Information Per Serving:
Calories 258 | Fat 9g |Sodium 994mg | Carbs 1g | Fiber 0.4g | Sugar 3g | Protein 16g

Seared Scallops

Prep Time: 15 minutes.
Cook Time: 6 minutes.
Serves: 4

Ingredients:

- 1 lb. large scallops
- Salt, to taste
- Black pepper, to taste
- 1 tablespoon olive oil
- 2 tablespoons butter
- 2 tablespoons parsley, chopped
- Lemon wedges, for serving

Preparation:

1. Season all the scallops with salt, balck pepper, and oil.
2. Melt butter and sear the scallops in a skillet for 3 minutes per side.
3. Drizzle parsley on top and garnish with lemon wedges.
4. Serve warm.

Serving Suggestion: Serve the scallops with lemon slices on top.

Variation Tip: Use white pepper for a change of flavor.

Nutritional Information Per Serving:
Calories 378 | Fat 21g |Sodium 146mg | Carbs 7.1g | Fiber 0.1g | Sugar 0.4g | Protein 23g

Thai Green Curry

Prep Time: 15 minutes.
Cook Time: 10 minutes.
Serves: 2

Ingredients:

- Fish
- 2 cod fillets
- 2 halibut fillets
- 2 snapper fillets
- 1 lemon
- 2 cups coconut milk
- 3 ounces baby spinach
- 2 ounces carrots, shredded

Preparation:

1. Add coconut milk and rest of the ingredients to a cooking pot.
2. Cook this mixture for 10 minutes on medium heat.
3. Serve warm.

Serving Suggestion: Serve the curry with white rice.

Variation Tip: Drizzle cheese on top for a rich taste.

Nutritional Information Per Serving:

Calories 351 | Fat 4g |Sodium 236mg | Carbs 19.1g | Fiber 0.3g | Sugar 0.1g | Protein 36g

Grilled salmon with Avocado Salsa

Prep Time: 15 minutes.
Cook Time: 10 minutes.
Serves: 4

Ingredients:

- 2 lbs. salmon, cut into 4 fillets
- 1 tablespoon of olive oil
- 1 teaspoon of salt
- 1 teaspoon of cumin
- 1 teaspoon of paprika
- 1 teaspoon of onion
- 1/2 teaspoon chili spices
- 1 teaspoon black pepper

Salsa:

- 1 avocado chopped
- ½ small red onion, sliced
- Juice of 2 limes
- 1 tablespoon of fresh coriander
- Salt, to taste

Preparation:

1. Mix all the spices in a bowl and rub over the salmon fillets along with olive oil.
2. Grill the salmon fillet for 5 minutes per side in a preheated grill.
3. Chopped avocados with rest of the ingredients in a bowl.
4. Serve the grilled fish with avocado mash on top.
5. Enjoy.

Serving Suggestion: Serve the salmon with sweet potato salad.

Variation Tip: Add some chopped bell pepper to the meal.

Nutritional Information Per Serving:

Calories 378 | Fat 7g |Sodium 316mg | Carbs 16.2g | Fiber 0.3g | Sugar 0.3g | Protein 26g

Lemon Garlic Cod with Tomatoes

Prep Time: 15 minutes.
Cook Time: 45 minutes.
Serves: 2

Ingredients:

- 1 ½ pounds cod
- 2 pints cherry tomatoes
- 2 tablespoons olive oil
- 1 teaspoon salt
- 3 garlic cloves, sliced
- 1 tablespoon fresh sage, chopped
- 2 lemons, sliced
- 2 tablespoons capers, for garnish

Preparation:

1. At 325 degrees F, preheat your oven.
2. Place cod in a greased 9x13 inches baking dish.
3. Add tomatoes, olive oil, garlic, sage, lemon and salt on top of the cod.
4. Bake the cod for 45 minutes in the oven.
5. Garnish with capers then serve warm.

Serving Suggestion: Serve the cod with roasted broccoli florets.

Variation Tip: Drizzle lemon zest on top before cooking.

Nutritional Information Per Serving:

Calories 415 | Fat 15g |Sodium 634mg | Carbs 14.3g | Fiber 1.4g | Sugar 1g | Protein 23.3g

Shrimp Pineapple

Prep Time: 15 minutes.
Cook Time: 15 minutes.
Serves: 4

Ingredients:

- 1 cup pineapple, chopped
- 1lb raw jumbo shrimp
- 1 ½ tablespoons arrowroot starch
- 2 tablespoons avocado oil

Sauce

- 1 tablespoon ginger, minced
- 2/3 cup pineapple juice
- 1 tablespoon garlic, minced
- 3 tablespoon sriracha
- 1 tablespoon soy sauce
- 2 teaspoons arrowroot starch
- 1 tablespoon garlic, minced

- 1 tablespoon honey
- 1/3 cup bell pepper, diced

Garnish

- Fresh green onion
- Sesame seeds
- Fresh limen

Preparation:

1. Mix all the sauce ingredients in a bowl and keep it aside.
2. Toss shrimp with arrowroot in a bowl and shake off the excess.
3. Set a skillet with olive oil over medium heat.
4. Stir in pineapple chunks and cook for 5 minutes.
5. Transfer to a plate and keep them aside.
6. Saute shrimp with avocado oil in the same skillet for 8 minutes.
7. Stir in bell peppers then saute for 1 minute.
8. Add prepared sauce and mix well.
9. Stir in pineapple juice and chunks.
10. Cook for 30 seconds then serve warm.

Serving Suggestion: Serve these shrimps with boiled white rice.

Variation Tip: Add garlic salt to the seasoning for more taste.

Nutritional Information Per Serving:

Calories 251 | Fat 17g |Sodium 723mg | Carbs 21g | Fiber 2.5g | Sugar 2g | Protein 7.3g

Fish Green Curry

Prep Time: 15 minutes.
Cook Time: 13 minutes.
Serves: 4

Ingredients:

- 1 (15-ounce can) coconut milk
- 2 tablespoons green curry paste
- 1 (1-inch) nub fresh ginger, peeled and grated
- 2 tablespoons lime juice
- 2 tablespoons fish sauce
- 1 crown broccoli, chopped
- 2 cups green beans, chopped
- 1 zucchini squash, chopped
- 2 pounds white fish
- Salt, to taste

Serving

- Coconut milk yogurt
- Chives

Preparation:

1. Add coconut milk, lime juice, fish sauce, ginger, and curry paste to a cooking pot and cook to a boil.
2. Stir in green beans and broccoli and cook for 3 minutes.
3. Stir fish and zucchnini, cover and cook for 10 minutes.
4. Serve warm.

Serving Suggestion: Serve the fish curry with cauliflower rice.

Variation Tip: Add olives or sliced mushrooms to the fish.

Nutritional Information Per Serving:

Calories 246 | Fat 15g |Sodium 220mg | Carbs 40.3g | Fiber 2.4g | Sugar 1.2g | Protein 12.4g

Vegan Meatballs

Prep Time: 20 minutes.
Cook Time: 48 minutes.
Serves: 4

Ingredients:

- 1 cup cooked quinoa
- 1 (15-ounce) can black beans
- 2 tablespoons water
- 3 garlic cloves, minced
- 1/2 cup shallot, diced
- 1/4 teaspoon salt
- 2 1/2 teaspoon fresh oregano
- 1/2 teaspoon red pepper flake
- 1/2 teaspoon fennel seeds
- 1/2 cup vegan parmesan cheese, shredded
- 2 tablespoons tomato paste
- 3 tablespoons fresh basil, chopped
- 2 tablespoons Worcestershire sauce

Preparation:

1. At 350 degrees F, preheat your oven.
2. Spread the beans in a baking sheet and bake for 15 minutes.
3. Meanwhile, sauté garlic, shallots and water to a skillet for 3 minutes.
4. Transfer to the food processor along with fennel, red pepper flakes, baked beans, oregano and salt.
5. Blend these ingredients just until incorporated.
6. Stir in quinoa, and rest of the ingredients then mix evenly.
7. Make golf-ball sized meatballs out of this mixture.
8. Spread these meatballs in a grease baking sheet and bake for 20-30 minutes until brown.
9. Flip the meatballs once cooked half way through.
10. Serve warm.

Serving Suggestion: Serve the meatballs with pita bread and chili sauce.

Variation Tip: Add chopped mushrooms to the batter as well.

Nutritional Information Per Serving:

Calories 338 | Fat 24g |Sodium 620mg | Carbs 58.3g | Fiber 2.4g | Sugar 1.2g | Protein 5.4g

Minestrone Soup

Prep Time: 15 minutes.
Cook Time: 40 minutes.
Serves: 6

Ingredients:

- 1 yellow onion, diced
- 3 garlic cloves, minced
- 1 carrot peeled and diced
- 4 celery stalks, diced
- 4 cups vegetable broth
- 1 (15-ounces) can of tomato juice
- 1 (15-ounces) can of diced tomatoes

- 8 ounces elbow pasta
- 1 (15ounces) can of red kidney beans rinsed and drained
- 1 (15ounces) can of white beans
- 2 handfuls baby spinach, chopped
- 1 teaspoon coriander
- 1 teaspoon oregano
- 1 teaspoon black pepper
- 1 teaspoon basil
- 1 teaspoon paprika
- Salt to taste
- Chopped parsley for garnish

Preparation:

1. Add carrot, garlic, celery, onion and vegetable broth in a cooking pot and cook for 20 minutes on a simmer.
2. Stir in rest of the ingredients and cook for 20 minutes.
3. Garnish with parsley.
4. Serve warm.

Serving Suggestion: Serve the soup with avocado salad.

Variation Tip: Add chopped mushrooms to the soup as well.

Nutritional Information Per Serving:
Calories 393 | Fat 3g |Sodium 510mg | Carbs 12g | Fiber 3g | Sugar 4g | Protein 4g

Tofu Fried Rice

Prep Time: 10 minutes.
Cook Time: 13 minutes.
Serves: 4

Ingredients:

- 1 package baked tofu
- 4 cup cauliflower rice
- 1 cup frozen peas
- 1 cup carrots, shredded
- 1 teaspoon onion powder
- 1 teaspoon garlic powder
- 1/2 cup soy sauce
- 1/4 cup scallions, chopped
- Salt and black pepper to taste

Preparation:

1. Saue tofu with peas, carrots, garlic powder, soy sauce, scallions, black pepper and salt in a cooking pan for 10 minutes.
2. Stir in cauliflower rice and mix well.
3. Cover and cook for 3 minutes on medium heat.
4. Serve warm.

Serving Suggestion: Serve the rice with kale salad.

Variation Tip: Add boiled couscous to the mixture.

Nutritional Information Per Serving:
Calories 378 | Fat 3.8g |Sodium 620mg | Carbs 13.3g | Fiber 2.4g | Sugar 1.2g | Protein 5.4g

Rice and Beans

Prep Time: 15 minutes.
Cook Time: 22 minutes.
Serves: 4

Ingredients:

- 1 cup dry brown rice
- 1 ½ cup water
- 1 can of black beans
- 1 teaspoon paprika
- 1 teaspoon garlic powder
- 1 teaspoon oregano
- 1 teaspoon cumin
- 1 teaspoon onion powder

Preparation:

1. At 350 degrees F, preheat your oven.
2. Add water and rice to the Instant Pot's insert.
3. Set a trivet over the rice and place a baking dish on top.
4. Add beans and rest of the ingredients to this bowl.
5. Cover and seal the lid and cook for 22 minutes at Low pressure.
6. Once done, release all the pressure and remove the lid.
7. Mix the beans and transfer to a serving plate.
8. Serve the beans with the rice.
9. Enjoy.

Serving Suggestion: Serve the beans with the spinach salad.

Variation Tip: Add crispy fried onion on top for better taste.

Nutritional Information Per Serving:

Calories 304 | Fat 31g |Sodium 834mg | Carbs 21.4g | Fiber 0.2g | Sugar 0.3g | Protein 4.6g

Corn Chowder

Prep Time: 15 minutes.
Cook Time: 28 minutes.
Serves: 8

Ingredients:

- 4 cups vegetable broth
- 8 cups corn
- 1 whole yellow onion, diced
- 1 tablespoon chili powder
- 1 teaspoon salt
- 4 cups water
- 1/4 cup nutritional yeast
- 1/4 lime juiced
- 1/4 cup cilantro

Preparation:

1. Add vegetable broth, onion, corn and chili powder to a cooking pot.
2. Cook for 8 minutes with occasional stirring.
3. Remove 1/3 of this cooking mixture and keep it aside.
4. Add water to the rest and cook for 20 minutes on a simmer.
5. Puree the cooked corn soup until smooth.

6. Stir in lime juice, yeast, and remaining corn mixture.
7. Serve warm with cilantro on top.
8. Enjoy.

Serving Suggestion: Serve the chowder with cauliflower salad.

Variation Tip: Top the chowder cheddar cheese with before serving.

Nutritional Information Per Serving:

Calories 341 | Fat 24g |Sodium 547mg | Carbs 36.4g | Fiber 1.2g | Sugar 1g | Protein 10.3g

Asian Slaw

Prep Time: 15 minutes.
Cook Time: 0 minutes.
Serves: 4

Ingredients:

Salad:

- 2 cups green cabbage, shredded
- 1/2 cup carrots, shredded
- 1/2 cup cilantro, chopped
- 1/2 cup bell peppers, sliced
- 1/2 cup peanuts, crushed
- Avocado slices

Dressing:

- 2 tablespoons peanut butter
- 1 teaspoon agave syrup
- 1 tablespoon soy sauce
- 1 teaspoon white wine vinegar
- 1 teaspoon lime juice
- 1 tablespoon water
- Salt and black black pepper to taste

Preparation:

1. First, mix all the dressing ingredients in a salad bowl.
2. Stir in rest of the slaw ingredients and mix well.
3. Serve.

Serving Suggestion: Serve the slaw with turkey burgers.

Variation Tip: Add some edamame beans to the bowl.

Nutritional Information Per Serving:

Calories 318 | Fat 15.7g |Sodium 124mg | Carbs 27g | Fiber 0.1g | Sugar 0.3g | Protein 4.9g

Spinach Alfredo Soup

Prep Time: 15 minutes.
Cook Time: 23 minutes.
Serves: 6

Ingredients:

- 2 cups cauliflower florets
- 1/2 teaspoon garlic, minced
- 1 teaspoon olive oil
- ½ cup cottage cheese
- 9 ounces shredded cheese

- 6 wedges Light Laughing Cow cheese
- ½ teaspoon salt
- ¼ teaspoon black pepper
- 1 cup cashew milk
- 26 ounces frozen Spinach
- 3 tablespoon Parmesan cheese, shredded
- 18 ounces yogurt

Preparation:

1. Boil cauliflower in a cooking pan filled with water for 10 minutes.
2. Traansfer the cauliflower florets to a blender along with 1 cup cooking liquid.
3. Puree this mixture and keep it aside.
4. Saute garlic with olive oil in
5. a suitable pan for 3 minutes.
6. Transfer to the cauliflower and add all these cheese, black pepper, milk and salt.
7. Blend these ingredients together until smooth.
8. Return the mixture to the saucepan and add one more cup of cooking liquid.
9. Cook the soup to a boil then add spinach and cook for 10 minutes.
10. Serve warm.

Serving Suggestion: Serve the soup with cauliflower rice.

Variation Tip: Add broccoli florets to the soup as well.

Nutritional Information Per Serving:
Calories 314 | Fat 2.2g |Sodium 276mg | Carbs 27.7g | Fiber 0.9g | Sugar 1.4g | Protein 8.8g

Artichoke Stuffed Mushroom

Prep Time: 15 minutes.
Cook Time: 20 minutes.
Serves: 8

Ingredients:

- 8 (1/2 ounces) Portobello Mushroom, caps

Filling ingredients:

- 1/4 cup alfredo sauce
- 2 wedges light laughing cow cheese
- 1 teaspoon garlic, minced
- 1 egg
- 4 ounces cheese, shredded
- 1-1/2 cup light cottage cheese
- 1/2 cup hearts of palm, diced
- 1 cup spinach, shredded
- 4 tablespoons parmesan, shredded

Preparation:

1. Mix all the filling ingredients in a suitable bowl.
2. Divide this mixture in the mushroom caps.
3. Place these stuffed caps in a greased baking sheet.
4. Bake them for 20 minutes at 350 degrees F in the oven.
5. Serve warm.

Serving Suggestion: Serve the mushrooms with kale salad.

Variation Tip: Add lemon zest and lemon juice for better taste.

Nutritional Information Per Serving:
Calories 324 | Fat 5g |Sodium 432mg | Carbs 13.1g | Fiber 0.3g | Sugar 1g | Protein 5.7g

Asparagus with Garlic

Prep Time: 15 minutes.
Cook Time: 45 minutes.
Serves: 4

Ingredients:

- 1 lb. thick asparagus spears, trimmed and chopped
- ½ cup garlic cloves, peeled and chopped
- 3 tablespoons olive oil
- Salt and black pepper, to taste

Preparation:

1. Mix asparagus with garlic, olive oil, black pepper and salt in a bowl.
2. Cover and marinate for 30 minutes.
3. Meanwhile, at 450 degrees F, preheat your oven.
4. Spread the asparagus in a baking sheet.
5. Roast them for 15 minutes in the preheated oven.
6. Serve warm.

Serving Suggestion: Serve the asparagus with toasted bread slices.

Variation Tip: Add boiled zucchini pasta to the mixture.

Nutritional Information Per Serving:
Calories 136 | Fat 10g |Sodium 249mg | Carbs 8g | Fiber 2g | Sugar 3g | Protein 4g

Avocado Tomato Salad

Prep Time: 15 minutes.
Cook Time: 14 minutes.
Serves: 2

Ingredients:

- 2 ripe avocados
- 2 ripe beefsteak tomatoes
- 2 tablespoons lemon juice
- 3 tablespoons cilantro, chopped
- Salt and black pepper to taste

Preparation:

1. Peel the avocados, remove their pits and cut into cubes.
2. Transfer the avocados to a salad bowl.
3. Stir in toamtoes, lemon juice, cilantro, black pepper and salt.
4. Mix well and serve fresh.

Serving Suggestion: Serve the salad with grilled salmon.

Variation Tip: Add canned corn to the salad.

Nutritional Information Per Serving:
Calories 151 | Fat 9g |Sodium 412mg | Carbs 43g | Fiber 0.3g | Sugar 1g | Protein 3g

5 & 1 Meal Plan

Week 1

Day 1:
Fueling Hacks:
Coffee Cake Muffins
Baked Kale Chips
Strawberry Yogurt
Brownie in a Tray
Dark Chocolate Mousse
Lean and Green Meal:
Lean Green Chicken Soup

Day 2:
Fueling Hacks:
Grilled Buffalo Shrimp
Strawberry Ice Cream
Banana Pudding
Banana Pops
Strawberry Cheesecake
Lean and Green Meal:
Avocado Chicken Salad

Day 3:
Fueling Hacks:
Taco Cups
Caprese Spaghetti Squash Nests
Fire Cracker Shrimp
Chia Seed Pudding
Crispy Zucchini Chips
Lean and Green Meal:
Chicken Pesto Pasta

Day 4:
Fueling Hacks:
Berry Quinoa
Celery Salad
Yogurt Trail Mix Bars
Curried Tuna Salad
Tuna Quinoa Cakes
Lean and Green Meal:
Sesame Chicken Fry

Day 5:
Fueling Hacks:
Banana Cookies
Oatmeal Pancakes
Taco Salad
Blueberry Muffins
Peanut Butter Cookies

Lean and Green Meal:
Teriyaki Chicken Broccoli

Day 6:
Fueling Hacks:
Celery Salad
Baked Kale Chips
Grilled Buffalo Shrimp
Curried Tuna Salad
Cranberry Sweet Potato Muffins
Lean and Green Meal:
White Chicken Chili

Day 7:
Fueling Hacks:
Cranberry Sweet Potato Muffins
Quinoa Bars
Tuna Quinoa Cakes
Buckwheat Crepes
Yogurt Trail Mix Bars
Lean and Green Meal:
Chicken Thighs with Green Olive

Week 2

Day 1:
Fueling Hacks:
Quinoa Pudding
Cranberry Sweet Potato Muffins
Baked Kale Chips
Grilled Buffalo Shrimp
Oatmeal Pancakes
Lean and Green Meal:
Chicken Divan

Day 2:
Fueling Hacks:
Cherry Dessert
Vanilla Pudding
Medifast Rolls
Sweet Potato Cheesecake
Cauliflower Breakfast Casserole
Lean and Green Meal:
Spicy Taco Meat

Day 3:
Fueling Hacks:
Curried Tuna Salad
Cranberry Sweet Potato Muffins

Quinoa Bars
Buckwheat Crepes
Celery Salad
Lean and Green Meal:
Beef Broccoli

Day 4:
Fueling Hacks:
Turkey Lettuce Wraps
Bell Pepper Bites
Avocado Shrimp Cucumber
Green Colada Smoothie
Pancetta Wrapped Prunes
Lean and Green Meal:
Ground Beef Salad

Day 5:
Fueling Hacks:
Queso Dip
Sweet Potato Rounds
Spinach Smoothie
Zucchini Bites
Medifast Patties
Lean and Green Meal:
Ground Beef Salad

Day 6:
Fueling Hacks:
Egg Cups
Lean and Green Smoothie
Green Apple Smoothie
Kale and Cheese Muffins
Matcha Avocado Smoothie
Lean and Green Meal:
Ground Beef Skillet

Day 7:
Fueling Hacks:
Baked Kale Chips
Grilled Buffalo Shrimp
Cranberry Sweet Potato Muffins
Buckwheat Crepes
Oatmeal Pancakes
Lean and Green Meal:
Green Beans with Pork and Potatoes

Week 3

Day 1:
Fueling Hacks:
Coffee Cake Muffins
Baked Kale Chips
Strawberry Yogurt

Brownie in a Tray
Dark Chocolate Mousse
Lean and Green Meal:
Roasted Shrimp and Green Beans

Day 2:
Fueling Hacks:
Grilled Buffalo Shrimp
Strawberry Ice Cream
Banana Pudding
Banana Pops
Strawberry Cheesecake
Lean and Green Meal:
Steak with Onions

Day 3:
Fueling Hacks:
Medifast Patties
Turkey Lettuce Wraps
Bell Pepper Bites
Avocado Shrimp Cucumber
Green Colada Smoothie
Lean and Green Meal:
Ground Beef Over Zoodles

Day 4:
Fueling Hacks:
Pancetta Wrapped Prunes
Peanut Butter Balls
Buckwheat Crepes
Goat Cheese Crostini
Buffalo Cauliflower
Lean and Green Meal:
Parmesan Shrimp Zoodles

Day 5:
Fueling Hacks:
Chia Seed Pudding
Quinoa Pudding
Yogurt Trail Mix Bars
Curried Tuna Salad
Tuna Quinoa Cakes
Lean and Green Meal:
Shrimp and Cauliflower Grits with Greens

Day 6:
Fueling Hacks:
Quinoa Pudding
Cranberry Sweet Potato Muffins
Quinoa Bars
Banana Cookies
Oatmeal Pancakes
Lean and Green Meal:

Salmon with Cherry Tomatoes

Day 7:
Fueling Hacks:
Cranberry Sweet Potato Muffins
Quinoa Bars
Tuna Quinoa Cakes
Buckwheat Crepes
Yogurt Trail Mix Bars
Lean and Green Meal:
Fish Pie

Week 4

Day 1:
Fueling Hacks:
Strawberry Cheesecake
Coffee Cake Muffins
Baked Kale Chips
Strawberry Yogurt
Brownie in a Tray
Lean and Green Meal:
Green Buddha Bowl

Day 2:
Fueling Hacks:
Quinoa Pudding
Celery Salad
Taco Salad
Yogurt Trail Mix Bars
Tuna Quinoa Cakes
Lean and Green Meal:
Turkey Broccoli

Day 3:
Fueling Hacks:
Cherry Dessert
Vanilla Pudding
Medifast Rolls
Sweet Potato Cheesecake
Cauliflower Breakfast Casserole

Lean and Green Meal:
Turkey Shepherds Pie

Day 4:
Fueling Hacks:
Oatmeal Pancakes
Baked Kale Chips
Grilled Buffalo Shrimp
Curried Tuna Salad
Celery Salad
Lean and Green Meal:
Chicken Zucchini

Day 5:
Fueling Hacks:
Cranberry Sweet Potato Muffins
Quinoa Bars
Banana Cookies
Oatmeal Pancakes
Taco Salad
Lean and Green Meal:
Chicken Piccata

Day 6:
Fueling Hacks:
Berry Quinoa
Celery Salad
Yogurt Trail Mix Bars
Curried Tuna Salad
Tuna Quinoa Cakes
Lean and Green Meal:
Braised Lamb Shanks

Day 7:
Fueling Hacks:
Baked Kale Chips
Grilled Buffalo Shrimp
Cranberry Sweet Potato Muffins
Buckwheat Crepes
Oatmeal Pancakes
Lean and Green Meal:
Green Lamb Curry

4 & 2 & 1 Meal Plan

Week 1

Day 1:
Fueling Hacks:
Apple Crisp
Avocado Shrimp Cucumber
Baked Kale Chips
Banana Cookies
Lean and Green Meals:
Artichoke Stuffed Mushroom
Asian Slaw
Snack:
½ cup peaches

Day 2:
Fueling Hacks:
Banana Pops
Banana Pudding
Bell Pepper Bites
Berry Quinoa
Lean and Green Meals:
Asparagus with Garlic
Avocado Chicken Salad
Snack:
¾ cup low-fat plain yogurt

Day 3:
Fueling Hacks:
Blueberry Muffins
Brownie in a Tray
Buckwheat Crepes
Buffalo Cauliflower
Lean and Green Meals:
Avocado Tomato Salad
Baked Chicken Stuffed
Snack:
4 ounces apple

Day 4:
Fueling Hacks:
Caprese Spaghetti Squash Nests
Cauliflower Bites
Cauliflower Breakfast Casserole
Celery Salad
Lean and Green Meals:
Baked Lemon Garlic Cod
BBQ Beef with Sweet Potato Salad
Snack:
3 celery stalks

Day 5:
Fueling Hacks:
Cherry Dessert
Chia Seed Pudding
Chocolate Cherry Cookie
Coffee Cake Muffins
Lean and Green Meals:
Beef Bake
Beef Broccoli
Snack:
½ cup fresh strawberries

Day 6:
Fueling Hacks:
Cranberry Sweet Potato Muffins
Crispy Zucchini Chips
Curried Tuna Salad
Dark Chocolate Mousse
Lean and Green Meals:
Beef Stew with Green Beans
Braised Lamb Shanks
Snack:
1 cup unsweetened cashew milk

Day 7:
Fueling Hacks:
Egg Cups
Fire Cracker Shrimp
Goat Cheese Crostini
Green Apple Smoothie
Lean and Green Meals:
Broccoli Chicken Casserole
Cauliflower Ground Beef Hash
Snack:
4 ounces orange

Week 2

Day 1:
Fueling Hacks:
Green Colada Smoothie
Grilled Buffalo Shrimp
Kale and Cheese Muffins
Lean and Green Smoothie
Lean and Green Meals:
Cauliflower Salad
Cheddar Turkey Burgers
Snack:
½ cup peaches

Day 2:
Fueling Hacks:
Matcha Avocado Smoothie
Medifast Patties
Medifast Rolls
Oatmeal Pancakes
Lean and Green Meals:
Chicken Chili
Chicken Divan
Snack:
¾ cup low-fat plain yogurt

Day 3:
Fueling Hacks:
Pancetta Wrapped Prunes
Peanut Butter Balls
Peanut Butter Brownie
Peanut Butter Cookies
Lean and Green Meals:
Chicken Pesto Pasta
Chicken Piccata
Snack:
4 ounces apple
Day 4:
Fueling Hacks:
Peanut Butter Cups
Queso Dip
Quinoa Bars
Quinoa Pudding
Lean and Green Meals:
Chicken Taco Soup
Chicken Thighs with Green Olive
Snack:
3 celery stalks

Day 5:
Fueling Hacks:
Spinach Smoothie
Strawberry Cheesecake
Strawberry Ice Cream
Strawberry Yogurt
Lean and Green Meals:
Chicken with Avocado Salsa
Chicken with Green Beans
Snack:
½ cup fresh strawberries

Day 6:
Fueling Hacks:
Stuffed pears with almonds
Sweet Potato Cheesecake
Sweet Potato Rounds

Taco Cups
Lean and Green Meals:
Corn Chowder
Creamy Scallops
Snack:
1 cup unsweetened cashew milk

Day 7:
Fueling Hacks:
Taco Salad
Tuna Quinoa Cakes
Turkey Lettuce Wraps
Vanilla Pudding
Lean and Green Meals:
Chicken Zucchini Boats
Chipotle Pork Loin
Snack:
4 ounces orange

Week 3

Day 1:
Fueling Hacks:
Yogurt Trail Mix Bars
Zucchini Bites
Caprese Spaghetti Squash Nests
Buckwheat Crepes
Lean and Green Meals:
Garlic Chicken with Zoodles
Goan Fish Curry
Snack:
½ cup peaches

Day 2:
Fueling Hacks:
Apple Crisp
Avocado Shrimp Cucumber
Baked Kale Chips
Banana Cookies
Lean and Green Meals:
Green Beans with Pork and Potatoes
Green Buddha Bowl
Snack:
¾ cup low-fat plain yogurt

Day 3:
Fueling Hacks:
Banana Pops
Banana Pudding
Bell Pepper Bites
Berry Quinoa
Lean and Green Meals:

Green Chicken Casserole
Green Lamb Curry
Snack:
4 ounces apple

Day 4:
Fueling Hacks:
Blueberry Muffins
Brownie in a Tray
Buckwheat Crepes
Buffalo Cauliflower
Lean and Green Meals:
Grilled Shrimp Kabobs
Ground Beef Over Zoodles
Snack:
3 celery stalks

Day 5:
Fueling Hacks:
Caprese Spaghetti Squash Nests
Cauliflower Bites
Cauliflower Breakfast Casserole
Celery Salad
Lean and Green Meals:
Lamb Pea Curry
Lean Green Chicken Soup
Snack:
½ cup fresh strawberries

Day 6:
Fueling Hacks:
Cherry Dessert
Chia Seed Pudding
Chocolate Cherry Cookie
Coffee Cake Muffins
Lean and Green Meals:
Lemon Garlic Cod with Tomatoes
Lemon Lamb Chops
Snack:
1 cup unsweetened cashew milk

Day 7:
Fueling Hacks:
Cranberry Sweet Potato Muffins
Crispy Zucchini Chips
Curried Tuna Salad
Dark Chocolate Mousse
Lean and Green Meals:
Lemon White Fish Fillets
Meatloaf
Snack:
4 ounces orange

Week 4

Day 1:
Fueling Hacks:
Egg Cups
Fire Cracker Shrimp
Goat Cheese Crostini
Green Apple Smoothie
Lean and Green Meals:
Medifast Chicken Fry
Mediterranean Beef and Rice
Snack:
½ cup peaches

Day 2:
Fueling Hacks:
Green Colada Smoothie
Grilled Buffalo Shrimp
Kale and Cheese Muffins
Lean and Green Smoothie
Lean and Green Meals:
Mexican Cauliflower Rice
Minestrone Soup
Snack:
¾ cup low-fat plain yogurt

Day 3:
Fueling Hacks:
Matcha Avocado Smoothie
Medifast Patties
Medifast Rolls
Oatmeal Pancakes
Lean and Green Meals:
Mojo Marinated Flank Steak
Pan Seared Beef and Mushrooms
Snack:
4 ounces apple

Day 4:
Fueling Hacks:
Pancetta Wrapped Prunes
Peanut Butter Balls
Peanut Butter Brownie
Peanut Butter Cookies
Lean and Green Meals:
Parmesan Shrimp Zoodles
Pepper Taco Bake
Snack:
3 celery stalks

Day 5:
Fueling Hacks:
Peanut Butter Cups

Queso Dip
Quinoa Bars
Quinoa Pudding
Lean and Green Meals:
Rice and Beans
Roasted Green Beans and Mushrooms
Snack:
½ cup fresh strawberries

Day 6:
Fueling Hacks:
Spinach Smoothie
Strawberry Cheesecake
Strawberry Ice Cream
Strawberry Yogurt
Lean and Green Meals:

Baked Chicken Stuffed
Pan Seared Beef and Mushrooms
Snack:
1 cup unsweetened cashew milk

Day 7:
Fueling Hacks:
Stuffed pears with almonds
Sweet Potato Cheesecake
Sweet Potato Rounds
Taco Cups
Lean and Green Meals:
Stuffed Chicken Breast
Halibut with Zucchini Noodles
Snack:
4 ounces orange

Conclusion

Are you ready to shed some pounds using the lean and green diet? Well, the whole approach mainly functions around the concept of calorie restriction. When you reduce your caloric intake, the body starts breaking down the existing reserves of glycogen and fats in the body to meet its need. This gradually helps in losing weight. According to the lean and green diet, the caloric intake should be around 1000 calories per day in order to initiate fat burning in the body. Since all diet plans suggesting such a drastic calorie cutdown omits a lot of food from the menu. You need to give up on a lot of things to keep your caloric intake this low. And this struggle of cutting down calories on a daily basis makes a dieter quit sooner than he planned to.

The lean and green diet, on the other hand, provides a perfect solution. It is easy and simple to follow because it offers the use of special powdered food known as fueling, which is made specially to keep the calories low and provide all the essential nutrients that are required to carry out the normal metabolic activities in the body. In simple words, it offers weight loss with good health, and you can manage to live on this diet without the fear of suffering from malnutrition or any nutritional deficiency. Each fueling is created to have only 100 to 110 calories, which is low enough to keep the daily caloric intake to 1000 calories.

Besides cutting down the caloric intake through the use of special fueling, the lean and green diet also aids weight loss through its "Lean and Green" meals. The diet is not all about Fuelings; rather, it gives you different options to enjoy actual food and its different flavors as well. As long as you are following the plan and eating lean and green food, you can expect to lose weight. It's about time that you put these recipes and the meal plan to practical use! Go for this diet plan and see its claimed benefits yourself. You will be surprised by the results!

Made in the USA
Coppell, TX
03 May 2021

54909354R00065